MAKING THE ULTIMATE DEMO

From the editors of
Electronic Musician magazine

• • •

Edited by Michael Molenda

Hal Leonard Publishing Corporation

© **1993 EMBooks**

Printed in Winona, Minnesota, USA

Library of Congress Catalog Card Number: 93-079750

This material has appeared previously in *Electronic Musician* magazine.

Production staff: Todd Souvignier, general manager; Peter Hirschfeld, series director; Ellen Richman, production director; Andy Jewett, assistant editor; Bob O'Donnell, contributing editor.
Design staff: Gelfand Graphic Design. Barbara Gelfand, art director.
Special thanks to Steve Oppenheimer for technical consultation, to Chris Albano and Brad Smith of Hal Leonard Publishing, and to the staff and freelance writers of *Electronic Musician*.

EMBooks
6400 Hollis Street, Suite 12
Emeryville, CA 94608
(510) 653-3307

Also from EMBooks:
Making Music With Your Computer
Electronic Musician's Tech Terms

Also from MixBooks:
Concert Sound
Sound For Picture
Music Producers
Hal Blaine and the Wrecking Crew
Auditory Perception Course

EMBooks and MixBooks are divisions of Act III Publishing.

ISBN 0-7935-2770-8

Contents

Introduction

I am a dinosaur. I don't mean that I wear bell bottoms and listen to disco-era Rod Stewart tracks—although, come to think of it, both Rod the Mod and bells are groovy again—but as far as music technology goes, I'm prehistoric.

When I joined my first band in 1974, a home studio was an impossible dream. There were no cassette ministudios offering multitrack recording to the masses for a few hundred bucks. If you wanted to make a demo, you booked time at a cheap commercial studio outfitted with a reel-to-reel 4-track machine. (Hey, it was good enough for *Sgt. Pepper*!) Unfortunately, great engineers rarely worked in these "demo dens," and the finished tracks were sonically inferior to the wonderful sounds on the LPs I bought at Tower Records. If you pined for aural majesty, you had to rob a bank and dump the money onto the lap of someone who owned a large state-of-the-art studio. (Just kidding!)

Today, everything is different. Technology now allows us to record master-quality tracks *at home*. Affordable digital multitracks, high-quality compact mixers, and digital multi-effects processors can turn a bedroom into The Record Plant, a garage into Abbey Road, or a living room into The Power Station. All you need is inspiration and some recording chops. That's where this book comes in.

Electronic Musician has always been committed to demystifying emerging music technologies. When the home re-cording boom went kapow, we expanded our coverage to help our readers exploit the multitrack medium. *Making the Ultimate Demo* is a compilation of some of these articles. But we didn't just toss a bunch of reprints together—this book is designed to be a comprehensive roadmap for the recording process.

We begin by helping you understand the vital components of a home studio. You'll learn about microphones, monitors, mixers, equipment maintenance, and more. Then it's session time. *Making the Ultimate Demo* offers tons of practical applications for recording specific instruments. There's even a section that reveals professional mixing techniques and explains popular effects such as reverb, delay, and pitch-shifting. And that's not all! We also let you peek inside some pro recording sessions and give you marketing tips for getting your music out of the studio and onto the charts.

About the only thing this book *can't* do is help you find your muse. But if you've got the inspiration covered, studying the following pages will definitely put you "on the track" towards recording absolutely slamming demos. Technology has dropped aural magic into your hot little hands; now, a sprinkle of practical recording knowledge is all you need to scare the hell out of those engineers and producers getting sloppy and fat in their expensive palaces of sound. So what are you waiting for? Read! Read! Read!

Michael Molenda

Foreword

Yes indeed, thrill seekers, you've come to the right place. As you know, there is a plethora of kicks in the record biz: Writing songs, performing to adoring masses, earning enormous quantities of money, and getting major cheese at glitzy awards shows.

But, to me at least, all of this pales next to the thrill of recording. Producing a great demo can be the most exciting part of the whole process of making records. (Excepting perhaps the fine celebratory cigar at the end of a session.) At the demo stage, a song is an innocent little unit ready to grow up to be anything you tell it to be. And right before your ears, it takes shape as the blueprint for a record.

I'm a big fan of getting a song recorded as soon as possible after it's written, because the more a demo retains whatever feeling went into the songwriting, the better.

Now, I don't mean to frighten you, but do you realize how gosh darn important these little tapes are to your career? For example, your demo must come across in just the right way or you won't excite a record company enough to sign your act, nor will an artist want to cover your song if you're a songwriter. And what, you might ask, *is* the right way? Well, allow me to reveal three bonehead pointers for making successful demos.

Pick a winner. There are many great singers and players out there, but make sure they are tuned into the style of your song. In other words, don't shop for country/western vocalists at your local opera house. If you're in a band, make sure all the members agree upon—and support—the group's stylistic niche before you set foot in the studio.

Flaunt your cheese. You've got to know your strengths. If your band is lucky enough to have a great singer, don't bury the vocal in the mix. If you're a songwriter looking to sell a song, make sure the *song* is heard instead of noodling musicians and a singer doing vocal gymnastics.

Hit 'em over the head. Your demo should leave no doubt in the listener's mind what you're all about. This is your calling card. Identity is king. If someone has to hypothesize about your stance or market, you're out!

Beyond following these hopefully helpful hints, making a great demo is simply a matter of capturing your spirit, heart, and soul on tape. And remember, most A&R folks listen for *music* on demos, not technical wizardry. Anyone with a budget can buy high gloss, but I'll take talent and imagination recorded direct-to-cassette over polished turds on 48-track digital any day. Go for the art of great performances. Keep it in the red and I'll see ya on the charts.

Scott Mathews

Scott Mathews, president of Totem Records, has produced Roy Orbison, Dick Dale, and Eddie Money, among others, and has had songs covered by such diverse artists as Dave Edmunds, Barbra Streisand, and The Tubes.

1

Getting Your Studio Together

Dream Home Studios

LANGUAGE IS WOEFULLY INARTICU-LATE when defining the mysteries of sound. One of legendary recording engineer Fred Catero's favorite war stories involves Carlos Santana's request for a guitar sound like a "flower opening up onto the sun." No recording school can tell you which button to push for *that* timbre.

Catero's anecdote illustrates the difficulty of getting a second party—a recording engineer, bandmate, or producer—to decipher someone's idea of a particular sound. Let's face it: Until mind-reading is included in the audio engineering curriculum, realizing an artist's aural desires will remain an exercise in experimentation and compromise. Some musicians deal with this sonic frustration by slamming recording engineers and blaming "the sound" for every rejected demo or missed hit, but the smart ones build home studios.

The home studio, or personal recording environment, is a den of liberation. Within its walls, nothing stands between the artist and the artist's vision except ingenuity and talent. In addition, the artist can configure the home studio to precisely complement his or her work habits. To further illustrate these benefits, I crashed the home studios of five diverse artists to discover how personal recording environments enhance their creativity.

THE BASEMENT STUDIO
AL EATON

"I set up my home studio primarily to record demos and have some fun, but it took on a life of its own," muses independent producer and remix artist Al Eaton. "The place has expanded into a full-blown 32-track studio with more equipment than some large commercial facilities."

Happily, Eaton's career has grown along with his studio. In addition to overstuffed equipment racks, Eaton's studio walls are adorned with gold and platinum records awarded for his engineering, remixing, and production expertise on albums by Too Short, Hammer, Ice-T, and other artists.

The studio, nestled in the basement of Eaton's tri-level home in the hills of El Cerrito, California, comprises a control room and a large, comfortable vocal booth. Because most of Eaton's projects are sequencer-based, live recording rooms were not a consideration when the studio was planned (although the vocal booth is certainly large enough to accommodate drums, guitar amps, and group background vocals for recording in separate passes).

by Michael Molenda

"I went house-shopping knowing that I'd be putting in a studio," says Eaton. "This place won out because it had a two-bridge view of the San Francisco Bay and an entire floor that could be turned into a studio without disturbing the rest of the house."

Because Eaton is at a career juncture where he can pick his projects, he isn't concerned with wigged-out artists rampaging through his living room. ("If I don't trust you, you don't work here.") However, making the studio more self-contained is a priority, and Eaton plans to add a separate entrance, kitchen, and bathroom.

"The main thing is being comfortable," he says. "I know I can do great work here (at home), because I know the equipment and the room and the sound. And anyway, where could I go and find this much equipment?"

ANNE HAMERSKY

Partial equipment list: Macintosh IIx and IIfx; Pacific Coast Technologies rack-mounted hard drives (30 MB to 2 GB); Digidesign *Sound Tools*, *Deck*, and *Sample Cell*; Mark of the Unicorn *Performer* and *Digital Performer*; Opcode *Vision* and *Studio Vision*; 360 Systems MidiPATCHER; KMX MIDI Central; Akai S1000HD; Roland JX-8P; Roland D-550; Roland U-220; Roland S-550; E-mu Proteus/1 and 2; Yamaha DX7; Korg EX-8000; Ensoniq SQ-R; Oberheim Matrix-1000; Alesis SR-16; Linn LM-1; Roland TR-808; DeltaLab Effectron JR 1050; Eventide H3000SE Ultra-Harmonizer; Yamaha REV-5; Yamaha SPX90II; Roland SRV-2000; Roland DEP-3; Orban 526A Dynamic Sibilance Controller; BBE 422A Sonic Maximizer; dbx 165 compressor/limiter (2); Furman QN-44 Quad Noise Gate (6); Soundtracs Quartz 48 x 24 x 48 mixer; Tascam ATR-80 2-inch 24- and 32-track recorders; Hafler PRO5000 power amp (2); Yamaha NS-10M, JBL 4412, and UREI 813 studio monitors; Panasonic SV-3500 and SV-3700 DAT recorders; Neumann U87A and AKG 414 B-ULS (3) microphones.

THE APARTMENT STUDIO
CLIFF MARTINEZ

A 13 x 25-foot studio apartment isn't exactly the live/work space you'd expect a successful film composer to inhabit. But the $270-per-month room in West Hollywood has housed Cliff Martinez through-

out his tenure as a drummer with the Red Hot Chili Peppers and Captain Beefheart, as well as housing the MIDI studio where he produced the film scores for *sex, lies, and videotape; Kafka;* and *Pump Up the Volume.*

"I'm a prisoner of rent control," admits Martinez. "When I moved here in 1976, the apartment was $135 per month. It's kind of hard to let go. You see, I've starved throughout most of my career, and I believe the secret of surviving one's devotion to music is to keep your overhead very low. Of course, the place has certain drawbacks. When the producer for *Kafka* came to visit, he was pretty shocked. It was like, 'You actually live here?' And I'm thinking, I guess it *is* a little claustrophobic having to sleep under my keyboard."

Al Eaton's basement studio is like an overflowing electronic toy shop.

Cliff Martinez inside the creative womb of his apartment MIDI studio.

IVY NEY

However, Martinez feels that the benefits of a comfortable acoustical environment more than compensate for the apartment's space limitations. In fact, Martinez is so happy in his creative womb that he recently acquired equipment that will allow him to record and mix future projects completely at home.

"Usually I sequence all the parts here and then transfer them to tape in a large studio," says Martinez. "Unfortunately, I always feel disoriented in the big studios because everything sounds a lot different than it does in my apartment. Also, it's very stressful trying to mix 40 cues in one week at commercial studio rates. When I mixed *Kafka*, I spent $25,000 in studio time in ten days. Today, for a fraction of that cost, I can *buy* gear that produces pro audio quality. So now I can simultaneously compose, record, and mix at home. When I get something I like, all I have to do is punch Record on the [mastering] deck."

To date, Martinez's film scores have not included acoustic instruments ("Everything comes out of a black box," he says), so recording and monitoring can be done at relatively low volumes. His consideration definitely lowers the threat of eviction. Even so, the apartment's thin walls are far from soundproof.

"I'm very lucky my neighbors are quite tolerant about hearing the same four measures of music repeated endlessly over 10-hour stretches," says Martinez.

Partial equipment list: Macintosh Quadra 700; PS Systems and Micronet 45 MB removable hard drives; Opcode *Vision;* Opcode Studio 5; JLCooper FaderMaster; Passport MIDI Transport; Kurzweil PX1000 synth; E-mu Proteus/2; Akai S1000 and Sequential Prophet 2000 samplers; E-mu SP-1200 sampling drum machine; KAT drumKAT; Roland Octapad; Lexicon PCM70 (2); Alesis QuadraVerb; Mackie 1604 mixer (2); Yamaha NS-10M studio monitors; Alesis ADAT; Sony TCD-10 Pro DAT recorder; Sony SLV-696HF VCR.

THE OFFICE STUDIO
RUSSELL BOND

"The recording environment doesn't limit the talent of a good engineer," says independent producer and co-owner of CornerMarket Productions, Russell Bond. "It always boils down to the talent of whomever is twiddling the knobs. Good engineers can record great tracks in unconventional places."

Bond should know. His "studio" is his office at the Music Annex recording complex in Menlo Park, California. Bond's hard-disk recording system is built into a rolling cabinet that can be wheeled into any number of acoustic environments, but many of the voice-overs used in his industrial video soundtracks are recorded right in the office.

"Actually, if the office was better soundproofed, I'd never need a conventional studio," says Bond. "Today, it doesn't really matter how many tracks you can record or what audio format you use. It comes down to whether you have a good listening environment or not. That's the critical factor in producing

great audio, and I'm comfortable with the sound of my office. The only problem is that I'm in the same area as the gear, so the (recorded) noise floor is sometimes masked by equipment hums and computer noises. The ideal monitoring environment would allow me the space to isolate the equipment better. But even so, all my post-production work is done right here, and I'm very proud of the sound quality."

Russell Bond at the "rolling" studio he keeps in his office.

Partial equipment list: Macintosh Quadra 950; Digidesign *Pro Tools* 8-track system; JLCooper CS10 MIDI console;

ANNE HAMERSKY

Summit Audio TPA200A dual tube pre-amp; Lexicon 300; Neumann U47 condenser microphone (2); AKG 460 microphone; Sony 2500 DAT modified with Apogee filters; Tannoy PBM 6.5 studio monitors.

THE BUNGALOW STUDIO
REEK HAVOK

Leave it to a drummer to construct an entire studio around a drum stool. When percussionist and sound designer Reek Havok decided to turn a detached 14 x 23-foot bungalow into a home studio, the ergonomics were determined by his playing position.

"I built the studio around a 'center of the universe' concept," says Havok. "Basically, everything is within arm's reach from my drum seat. I can spin around and work at the Macintosh, or the mixer, or the keyboard controller. My monitor speakers are hung from the ceiling and tilted at a 45-degree angle so I can hear them at each position."

Originally, the system was composed of an electronic drum kit hooked up to a Macintosh. However, Havok's increasing success as a sound designer necessitated the acquisition of more MIDI and recording gear. "Everything kept evolving around the circle," he says.

The natural evolution did not extend to the bungalow itself, which was renovated to provide suitable sound isolation. The interior was stripped down and replaced with insulated double walls, and the window—which Havok wanted for natural air and sunlight—was soundproofed with two sliding, double-glazed glass plates.

"You do whatever it takes to produce great sounds, but it seems easier to break the rules when you're the lord of the manor, so to speak," says Havok. "For instance, when I worked on a rave [dance] track for Fiorella Terenzi using sampled radio waves from her *Sounds of the Universe* CD, I played drum samples on the keyboard instead of my electronic kit and performed keyboard pads on the drums, because my sticks are faster than my fingers. Who's going to know?"

Reek Havok surrounded by his "drummer ergonomic" studio gear.

Partial equipment list: Macintosh IIx with 8 MB RAM and 170 MB hard disk; Digidesign *Sound Tools;* Opcode *Studio Vision;* Lone Wolf MIDITap (3); JLCooper SyncMaster; Dynacord ADD-Two sampler; E-mu Emulator IIIxs; E-mu Proteus MPS; Kawai K1; Yamaha DX9; E-mu Proteus/1, 2, 3, and ProCussion; Simmons SDE; E-mu SP-1200 sampling drum machine; Lexicon PCM 41; Ibanez HD-1000 Harmonizer; Dynacord DRP-20; DigiTech DSP256XL; Roland SRV-2000; Marshall 9000 guitar preamp; KAT drumKAT and MIDI Mallet Controller; custom "Reek Havok" drum pads; Dynacord MCX 16 x 4 x 2 mixer; Yamaha 1602 submixer; BGW 250B and UREI 6290 power amps; JBL 4410 studio monitors; JBL 4699B Cabaret loudspeakers; Sony DTC-700 DAT recorder.

THE MOBILE HOME STUDIO
JON PLUTTE

"I was sick and tired of getting hung up by technology," says Jon Plutte, guitarist and songwriter for up-and-coming alternative country duo Bolshoi Rodeo. "For years I was a prisoner of my Macintosh, my MIDI gear, and a sequencing program. I finally realized that I was messing with machines instead of writing music."

To focus more on composing, Plutte sold his MIDI studio and replaced it with a simple "songwriter's system." The revised studio fit perfectly against a living-room wall inside the mobile home he shares with his wife and son. Renovations were limited to construction of an equipment cabinet and a mixer/recorder desk.

"The simplicity of the system allows me to do what I do best, which is play guitar and write songs," says Plutte. "Also, because I'm working in a familiar place, all the recording parameters are second nature. I know where to place the vocal mic to get the best sound and how to preset my guitar levels. Everything is set up so that nothing interferes with getting song ideas on tape, and the living room provides a cozy recording environment."

The sketchbook system matches the organic method that Plutte and Bolshoi partner and singer/songwriter Denise Bon

Partial equipment list: Tascam 488 Portastudio; Harmon Kardon HK395i power amp; Boston Acoustics A60 stereo speakers; JBL Control SB-1 subwoofer; Alesis SR-16 drum machine; JLCooper PPS-1 synchronizer; ART Multiverb; dbx 363X Dual Gate; Mesa/Boogie Caliber 22 guitar amp; Shure SM57LC dynamic microphone.

PERSONAL BEST

As you can see, a "dream" home studio is just about any system that allows an artist the freedom to produce better work. It's as simple as that. For Al Eaton, this means having a virtual toy store of technology, while Jon Plutte desires only basic documentation gear.

At its highest technical level, a home studio empowers the creator to deter-

ANNE HAMERSKY

Jon Plutte cuts tracks while relaxing at home.

Giovanni use to develop songs. "Stupid" drum tracks are programmed to establish tempos, and time code is recorded to facilitate revising the percussion after the bass and guitar parts are tracked.

"We generally go around and around in circles until the song feels right," explains Plutte. "It's kind of like sculpture. We keep chipping away until the right performances and ideas are discovered."

mine the end product—a perk that, until fairly recently, remained the province of commercial recording facilities. Society can only be enriched by audio productions that are nurtured, beginning to end, by talented and visionary artists. Why shouldn't musicians be as self-sufficient as painters, who surely do not need, or want, an intermediary to mix the colors awaiting the canvas? ●

Maximizing Your Mixer

NOBODY BOUGHT ME A 72-INPUT NEVE VR-series mixing console for my birthday, so I'll have to make do with the lesser model currently residing in my studio. Similarly, I'm sure many of you drive affordable (and sensible) Tercels, rather than luxurious (and snobby) BMWs. But employing a modest console in no way dooms my studio to turn out harsh-sounding, noisy masters. After all, a good driver in a Tercel is a safe chauffeur, while a bad driver in a Beamer is a menace, albeit a comfortable one.

In the typical home studio, the choice of mixer often is dictated by price. Fiscal compromises usually rate the model with just enough features (i.e., no frills) the winner. For example, MIDI musicians often emphasize quantity of mixer inputs over features such as parametric EQ.

In high-ticket consoles, the money tends to go towards highly refined circuitry for critical functions such as microphone preamps and equalizers, as well as quality connectors and pots. Modern technology allows manufacturers to expand features and save money by compromising on circuit sophistication and component quality. Sometimes the most inexpensive console sounds good if pushed to its peak performance. The bottom line is to identify weak spots and find ways to avoid them.

PRIME POSITION

The best place to start is the placement and connection of your mixer. Avoid putting the mixer near any source that radiates magnetic or radio-frequency waves, such as power amplifiers, speakers, computers, digital signal processors, or video monitors. The most sensitive area of the mixer is near the top of the channel strip where the input preamps are located, as they provide the highest gain.

Be sure your mixer has a solid ground and clean AC power, or you may end up with noise and distortion that can't be eliminated. Neatness counts: Careful wiring and quality cable make a drastic difference in the number of hums, buzzes, and assorted nasty noises the system picks up. Using balanced inputs whenever possible helps avoid these problems, and minimizes ground loops too. Direct boxes provide the easiest method of balancing signals.

GAIN STRUCTURING AND NOISE

Once the mixer is situated and hooked up, the most critical aspect of the sonic performance in virtually any *by Larry the O* audio chain is gain structuring. Careful gain structuring minimizes the noise and distortion that identifies an amateur demo tape. A signal passing through a typical mixer traverses at least three gain stages: the preamp, the summing buses, and the output section. Typically, each of these stages offers a level control: a preamp trim (usually found at the top of the channel strip), a channel fader, and a master fader.

The preamp section of the mixer has the most gain, and its behavior largely dictates the gain structure. Some preamps are noisy when turned up near maximum, while others are noisiest when set low. This may be due to a combination of component quality, shielding, grounding, and topology. (Some preamp trims are attenuators that act on the signal before, or even after, a fixed-gain op-amp stage, while others are in the feedback loop of the op-amp, varying the circuit's gain.) The objective is to familiarize yourself with the noise and distortion characteristics of the different stages and find optimal settings.

To get a feel for your system's quiescent noise (noise level with no signal), turn the mixer preamp trim all the way down, leave the EQ flat, and set the channel and master faders at about 70 percent. Listen closely to the noise level as you slowly raise the preamp trim, to see if there is a particular spot where noise takes a jump (often in the last 10 percent of the pot's rotation). Since this test requires high monitor levels to reveal subtle noise differences, exercise extreme caution: One tiny pop can destroy your speakers (as well as your ears).

CLIPPING

The most common preventable source of distortion in inexpensive mixers is clipping. This occurs when the circuit runs out of available headroom, so it is important to know the dynamic limits of your mixer's gain stages. Put a signal from a test oscillator, or a simple, steady tone from a synthesizer (a sine wave is ideal), calibrated to the mixer's specified nominal input level, into a channel and perform the same exercise used to check quiescent noise levels. As you increase the gain, be careful to lower channel or master fader levels as necessary to avoid overloading any stage other than the one being tested. Listen closely for the first hint of distortion. While listening for distortion, watch any level indicators (channel overload LEDs and channel or master meters) to get an idea of the correlation between their readings and the aural onset of distortion.

A single tone isn't a comprehensive test, as practical use often requires multiple sources to be routed through the mixer simultaneously. While this operation has no effect on the individual preamps, the summing buses are impacted, as each individual signal contributes noise and reduces headroom. Channel faders, and occasionally even preamp trims, may need to be adjusted to avoid overloading summing buses and master output stages.

When tracking, less is often more. If your mixer has direct channel outputs,

PAUL RIDER

feeding your tape deck from those eliminates several stages of electronics and the accompanying noise and distortion.

EQUALIZATION

Moving beyond the primary issues of noise and headroom, the next most pressing concern about mixers is the sound of the equalization. Circuit design and component quality are the determinants here. Most inexpensive mixers offer simple EQ, such as fixed two-band shelving (treble and bass), fixed three-band (treble, bass shelving, midrange peaking), or three-band with switchable (or sweepable) midrange. If you are lucky (or paid more), you may get switchable/sweepable high and/or low frequencies, or more bands.

As with gain structuring, you need to learn the characteristics of the EQ to optimize its use. Identify the center frequencies, check the amount of boost and cut available, and find the slope of the shelving and the bandwidth of the peaking filters. One often-overlooked concern is

Peter Gabriel with the custom SSL console built for his Real World studio near Bath, England.

that boosting the EQ increases the signal level, which can cause clipping. In most cases, cutting undesired frequencies is preferable to boosting desired ones. Having said that, it is important to note that the equalization of some mixers sounds thin or wimpy when set flat and sounds much better when some boost is applied.

THE IN CROWD

For many of us, getting the most out of a mixer is affected by how much we can get into it. While analyzing the block diagram for the Ramsa 8118, I discovered that selecting Monitor on the switchable, stereo, post-fader monitor/effects send connected the channel line inputs to this send, even when the microphone input was selected by the mic/line switch. Taking the outputs of this send bus and connecting them to the master sub-inputs, I was able to use the eighteen line inputs simultaneously with the mic inputs, albeit with no channel facilities such as EQ.

Since many synthesizers include on-board signal processing and panning, effects returns are useful for more than just effects. I commandeered the effects returns and other sub-inputs to bring more line signals into the board and was able to get more than 40 inputs for mixdown on Ramsa's ostensibly 18-input mixer. And if effects-return knobs seem more difficult to mix with than faders, remember that you can use your sequencer to automate levels of MIDI synths, samplers, and effects.

AUDIO SUPPLEMENTS

Another way to get the most out of your mixer is by selectively supplementing it. Many inexpensive mixers sound pretty good except for their mic preamps, which usually are terrible. Purchasing an inexpensive outboard mic preamp allows for much better-sounding vocal or acoustic instrument tracks at an investment of only a few hundred dollars. Similarly, buying one or two inexpensive parametric EQs will let you treat critical signals better than the limited EQ your mixer may have.

Not enough effects sends? Some multi-effects processors have stereo inputs that are summed to mono before processing.

I've taken advantage of this by routing direct outs from two separate mixer channels into a signal processor and letting the box do the mixing. This little trick also saves your effects sends for more critical applications. Don't have direct outs? If your mixer has insert points, a Y-adapter (with one end going back into the insert and the other to wherever you wish) effectively turns an insert into a direct out.

If you plan to get into creative patching, you may find it useful (if somewhat costly) to connect a patch bay to your mixer's ins and outs. Although it can be a pain to wire, a patch bay saves wear and

Compact mixers, such as Mackie Designs' CR-1604, can be life-savers when space is at a premium.

tear on the mixer's connectors and eliminates the need to crawl around the back of the mixer. Be sure to construct a patch bay that services *all* your mixer's inputs and outputs, even if it ends up being a lot of jacks. Halfway measures work fine, but if you worship at the altar of "kludge patching," you'll eventually want access to even the most obscure patch points.

MASTER FADE

Many musicians and engineers recoil at the mere thought of crawling into schematics, but all your efforts will be repaid when you save a brutal mix with some inspired patching. In many ways, getting optimum performance from a mixer is no different than dragging an incendiary solo from a laconic guitarist—you need to pull a few tricks from your sleeve. The rewards of learning all these tricks go far beyond the tapes you make now, because the same approach and tricks are used by every engineer on every level of console, right up to the Neve I'll see on my *next* birthday. ●

The Ins and Outs of Patch Bays

SO YOU'VE ADDED ANOTHER SIGNAL PROCESSOR to a rack crammed with effects boxes, all of which are needed for your next mixdown. Unfortunately, too many signals are vying for precious few mixer inputs. Your outboard gear finally has overrun the capabilities of your recording system. But don't get mad, get a patch bay.

A patch bay is a sonic traffic controller. Outboard effects and mixer functions (such as input channel inserts and direct sends) are wired into a mechanical routing system that allows audio signals to be sent from one place to another via cables plugged into the appropriate jacks. Once these patch points are wired and labeled, signals can be routed easily to outboard signal processors without climbing behind consoles and effects racks. Obviously, this is a major ergonomics boon to the embattled recording engineer. Patch bays also are useful for tracing signal-path problems and providing options to work around them.

SYSTEM CONFIGURATIONS

We can thank Ma Bell for developing the mechanical and electrical switching systems for telephones that were forerunners of the patch bays used in today's recording studios. (I'm sure you've seen old movies where telephone operators connect calls by plugging long cables into a switchboard.)

Several types of patching systems are used for recording. The most common are TT (Tiny Telephone, also called "Bantam") and ¼-inch connectors, but patch bays are available with a wide assortment of military, telephone, and ¼-inch TRS stereo jacks.

TTs are the small-holed (0.173-inch) patch bays that service large studios, while ¼-inch systems are considered semi-professional. The major differences between the formats are size and application. For instance, a ¼-inch patch bay housed in a single-rackspace configuration can fit 32 to 48 jacks, while a TT system crams 96 jacks into the same space. In a pro studio, where nearly every piece of equipment is wired into the patch bay, the space-saving TT system is essential.

TT jacks can be wired as balanced lines, but it's difficult to find balanced ¼-inch patch bays. Fortunately, unbalanced systems can be relatively noise-free. Balanced lines offer common-mode re- *by Neal Brighton* jection, where unwanted noise cancels itself out, but a carefully wired unbalanced system (high-quality shielded wire, short cable runs, and so on) ensures reasonable sound quality. In addition, most modern gear conforms to a standard of high-impedance inputs and low-impedance outputs which diminishes noisy impedance mismatches.

PATCH POINTS

There are connections on both the front and back of a patch bay. The rear connectors are the permanent links to the various pieces of gear, while you make on-the-spot routing changes via the *patch points* (the front panel jacks).

Normalled patch bays are wired such that a signal is internally routed from one permanently attached device to a predetermined, permanently attached point without requiring a patch cable (**Fig. 1**). If a cable is plugged into either front-panel jack (**Fig. 2**), the internal connection (the "normal" signal path) is interrupted and the signal goes to the cable instead of following the prewired path. While not a patch bay *per se*, a console insert point is a good example of a normalled connection.

In patch bays that are not normalled, all signal routing is done at the front panel. If you want to route a signal from an Aux 2 send to a reverb, you have to use a patch cord to connect the front-panel Aux 2 Out to the Reverb In. Not surprisingly, unnormalled patch points commonly are used to access outboard gear such as noise gates, delays, and reverb units.

To simplify home studio operations, I often normal (or dedicate) an aux send from the mixer to the input of a reverb unit. This makes mixing easy, since Aux 2 always is Reverb A. No patching is necessary. During tracking, if I want to feed a guitar directly into Reverb A, I simply break the normal on the patch bay with the guitar cord. The connection with the aux send is cut off, and the guitar is routed directly into Reverb A. Without the benefit of a patch bay, the engineer would have to disconnect the aux send cable and replace it with the guitar cord.

If you don't want the signal to disappear when a patch cord is inserted, you can use *half-normalled points*. These continue to route signal through the patch bay even when broken by a patch cord (**Fig. 3**). Half-normalled points are useful because they allow the engineer to "Y" a signal to two different locations.

SYSTEM SELECTION

Deciding which patch bay to use for your personal recording system sometimes comes down to a matter of free time.

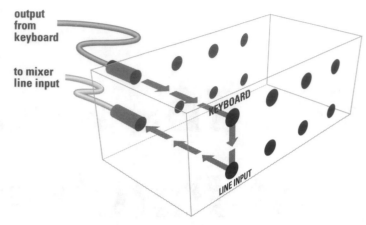

FIG. 1
A normalled patch point.

Most TT systems are wired via solder lugs or terminal blocks, and these require eons of wiring time to set up. However, one of the advantages of all this work is that you can wire normalled or unnormalled patch points wherever you need them.

Cost is another factor. While the price difference between TT and ¼-inch patch-bay frames is negligible, cable costs are another matter. TT patch cables cost approximately ten dollars each. If you have a large patch bay, the patch cords alone can cost hundreds of dollars (just count all those signal processors you own!).

Since most semi-pro recording gear runs at -10 dBV with unbalanced lines, ¼-inch patch bays offer home studios a lot of advantages. First, the patch cables are inexpensive and easy to make. The price of one TT cord buys several ¼-inch cables. On top of that, the rear panels of most ¼-inch patch bays are prewired

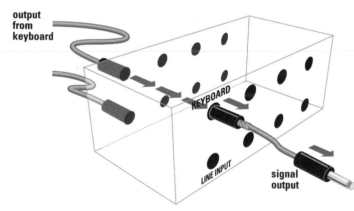

FIG. 2
To reroute a signal path, the user "breaks" the normal with a patch cable.

with RCA or ¼-inch jacks. Since ¼-inch jacks (both balanced *and* unbalanced) are the standard for most musical instruments, you're already wired and ready to go. You spend less time soldering and more time making music.

Unfortunately, every manufacturer configures their prewired patch bays differently, so exercise care when shopping. For example, Tascam makes ¼-inch patch bays in rows of sixteen, while ProCo offers a similar frame with rows of 24. In addition, some manufacturers make it easy to switch prewired points between normalled and unnormalled, while others make it nearly impossible. So before you buy a prewired model, make sure it offers the flexibility you need.

A final note about ¼-inch patch bays: They're heavy. When row upon row of cable is connected to the back of the patch bay, the combined weight can pull the plugs right out of the jacks. Make sure all of your cables are bound and secured so that the weight of the cables is off the plugs. This precaution saves tons of headaches later on. And if your reverb return is silent, make sure the patch cable is connected before tearing apart your entire system.

THE CASE FOR NORMALCY

The next big patch-bay decision is which lines should be normalled. It depends on how you like to work. If you are a heavy-duty MIDI person, you may want to normal your keyboards (and sound modules) to the line inputs of your mixing board. This means your sampler always comes up on Channel 1, your keyboard synth on Channel 2, and so on. However, you also have the flexibility (through the patch bay) to route your sampler elsewhere, as needed.

For musicians who like to walk into their studios and have everything ready to go, I recommend normalling mixer aux sends to often-used signal processors. It's a joy to simply twist a knob for reverb, instead of having to constantly patch cables into effects boxes. Also, because channel inserts are great for putting gates and compressors into the signal path, it makes sense to have them easily accessible on the patch bay. If you want even more flexibility, patch up your direct outputs.

Another useful spot for normalled points is the stereo bus. An easy setup for mixdowns is to normal, or half-normal,

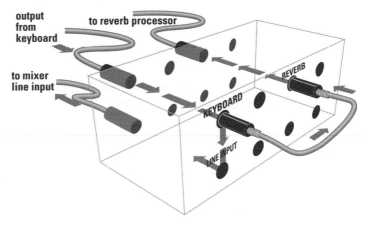

output from keyboard

to reverb processor

to mixer line input

REVERB

KEYBOARD

LINE INPUT

the inputs of your mastering deck to the stereo bus, automatically routing the stereo bus signal into the mastering deck; the deck's outputs are normalled back to available mixer returns for monitoring. This way, you're always ready to mix.

PATCHED OUT

A properly wired (and labeled) patch bay makes your hours in the studio much more fun and productive. With countless signal-routing options at your fingertips, a patch bay saves time and energy that is better directed towards music-making. After all, I'm sure most musicians agree that crawling behind mixers and effects racks is *not* a creative process. •

FIG. 3
A half-normalled patch point.

The Monitoring Milieu

"PENNY WISE, POUND FOOLISH," warns the old adage. That principle certainly applies to home studio engineers who reference music tracks on consumer stereo speakers; the sound from these speakers often is a far cry from audio reality. Although there's no law against mixing or recording in an aural fantasy world (some musicians prefer it), you should be aware of the fundamental differences distinguishing common hi-fi speakers from professional studio reference monitors.

The basic function of a studio monitor is to faithfully reproduce an incoming signal without adding coloration or changing the character or tonal balance of the sound. On the other hand, the average home stereo speaker is designed to make music sound as good as possible, often by emphasizing certain frequencies that make it stand out from the rest of the pack (especially during that all-important five-minute audition in the sales showroom). A little zing in the high frequencies and some extra punch in the bass may sell speakers, but these so-called enhancements sabotage audio accuracy.

And there's the rub. If your speakers don't provide an accurate reproduction of what's on tape or what's coming out of the console, it's difficult to make decisions concerning instrument and patch selection, equalization, or the balance of elements during mixdown. In addition, commercial playback systems range from 3-inch television speakers to elaborate audiophile installations. To ensure that overall instrumental and vocal balances remain consistent, it's essential that your speakers "translate" well to any system, large or small.

ACOUSTIC PERCEPTION

Consistent mixes require a critical listening environment. So don't wheel some 7-foot, 1,400-pound monster monitors into your studio, stand them against a far wall, and pump up the volume. This live sound-system approach is a bad idea: As the sound-source-to-listener distance is increased, a blend results as the original sound mixes with the acoustical effects of the room. Echoes and reverberation occur as sounds reflect off walls, furniture, floor, and ceiling.

Psychoacoustically, this approach creates a number of problems, as the listener's brain attempts to sort out the differences *by George Petersen* between the direct sound and an endless *melange* of unwanted room reflections. Unless your studio budget includes a hefty allotment for studio designers and acousticians, you're stuck creating music in a less-than-perfect environment. An effective and inexpensive solution is listening to monitor speakers in the *close-* or *near-field* (approximately one meter away), which increases the ratio of direct-to-reflected sound, greatly reducing the effects of poor room acoustics.

However, not all studio monitors are practical for near-field applications. Since listening is done at close quarters, it's important that the combined image of the drivers be coherent at short distances. Systems designed for near-field applications have closely spaced drivers or employ a coaxial-type design, where the high-frequency drivers are located on the same axis as the woofers. Another approach employs two small mid-/high-frequency cabinets (satellites) combined with one or two subwoofer enclosures that are located several feet from the satellites.

MONITOR PLACEMENT

Because near-field reference monitors can reduce unwanted acoustical effects within the listening space, speaker placement is critical. Position your speakers with the high-frequency elements at ear level and each monitor aimed slightly inward. This creates a sweet spot where the listener is precisely on-axis with the monitor. The most accurate perception of sound is attained within this position, because the sonic character of many speakers changes dramatically when heard off-axis.

This phenomenon, known as *off-axis coloration*, can be demonstrated by referencing a sound while facing the monitor and comparing that to the sound heard after taking a step to either side of the same monitor. Typical symptoms of off-axis coloration are a loss of high-frequency information or a change in the midrange characteristics. Since low-frequency information is largely non-directional, bass response generally is unaffected by off-axis listening.

A LOOK AT MONITOR DESIGNS

There are any number of ways to mount speakers in a cabinet, but most enclosures designed for music reproduction fall into two basic categories: *sealed* and *vented*.

Sealed designs (usually known as acoustic-suspension types) have the speaker components mounted on the outside of an airtight cabinet, which prevents the escape of air displaced by the woofer's rearward

motion. Increased air pressure within the cabinet acts as a springboard to push the woofer's cone forward.

Vented systems (sometimes called bass-reflex systems) have one or more openings that create a small amount of phase cancellation at the woofer's resonant frequency while increasing bass response at a lower frequency. (The resonant frequency is the point where a speaker's mechanical efficiency is at its highest level, as determined by the size, mass, and stiffness of the speaker cone.)

These openings (called vents or ports) can be mounted on the front or rear of the speaker enclosure. When rear-vented monitors are placed near walls or other sound-reflecting surfaces, the sound waves exiting the port are directed elsewhere in the room. Occasionally this cre-

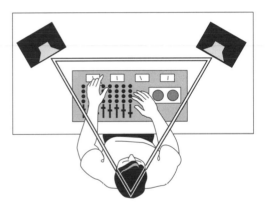

ates an unpredictable situation in which the direct sound from the woofers reaches the listener's ears a few milliseconds earlier than the reflected signal, often resulting in emphasized bass frequencies. In some instances, the net effect can be a *loss* of bass response, if the reflected signal is out of phase with the direct sound.

A number of speaker manufacturers employ coaxially mounted speakers, usually consisting of some sort of tweeter or other high-frequency unit mounted in the center of a bass reproducer. Coaxial speakers give the impression that sound is coming from a single point source, which improves coherence at close listening distances.

For more than 50 years, speaker designers have debated the question of the "right" number of components in a loudspeaker system, and still no apparent solution is in sight. Obviously, no single

A recommended starting position for close-field monitor placement.

speaker faithfully reproduces the entire audio spectrum. The concept of dividing the load of audio reproduction among many specialized drivers is a good idea. However, each crossover network that routes sound to its respective driver introduces a certain amount of phase error. The physical realities of near-field monitoring limit the number of drivers that can be clustered together to produce a coherent sound image at a close listening distance. Therefore, most compact studio monitors are two- or three-way systems.

SPEAKER SPECS

The most important specification of a loudspeaker system is *frequency response*, the range of frequencies a loudspeaker can reproduce. Unfortunately, this figure is virtually useless unless combined with some sort of *tolerance* specification (often expressed as something like ±3 dB). An ideal loudspeaker system offers "flat" response, which occurs when all frequencies are reproduced at a constant level.

However, keep in mind that a 3-inch transistor radio speaker theoretically could have a frequency response of 20 Hz to 20 kHz. What's left out is the fact that its *actual* frequency response could be -100 dB at the extreme ends of the scale. Since every 10 dB of change represents a doubling (or halving) in perceived volume, the amount of 20 Hz energy reproduced by the 3-inch speaker is infinitesimally small.

A speaker's overall efficiency is indicated by a *sensitivity* rating, which is expressed as the sound pressure level (in decibels) the speaker produces, given a 1-watt input, measured at one meter. Since console-mounted speakers usually are heard from a distance of around one meter, the sensitivity rating is important. Sensitivity ratings for loudspeakers range from about 80 dB to more than 100 dB.

What does this all mean in real terms? Let's say your monitor has a sensitivity spec of 90 dB. Since each 10 dB volume increase requires ten times more amplifier power, we can determine that your monitor provides 100 dB from a 10-watt input or 110 dB from a 100-watt input. (Because the scale is based on a logarith-

mic progression, we also know that each volume increase of 3 dB requires a doubling of amplifier power.) By combining this knowledge of sensitivity with a monitor's maximum power-handling capacity, you can tell if a given monitor is loud enough to suit your needs.

OTHER FEATURES

Removable front grilles are a plus. While many grille materials are "acoustically transparent," other problems stem from diffraction effects and edge reflections caused when sounds from the high- and mid-frequency drivers bounce off the wood or plastic grille frame.

On the rear of the speaker, input terminals range from screw fasteners to gold-plated, five-way binding posts. The latter accommodate banana plugs, spade lugs, test prods, and bare wires bent to go around the post, and also have holes in the post itself for inserting various gauges of speaker wire. If you frequently change speakers in your studio, banana connectors make a lot of sense, as they provide a solid and easily removable connection.

Yamaha's inexpensive NS-10M monitors are found in hundreds of studios throughout the world, and have become the unofficial reference standard.

Computer and video monitors are commonplace in today's electronic music studio. Because of this, many reference speakers provide internal magnetic shielding to reduce or eliminate the picture distortion that occurs whenever a large magnetic structure is placed near a video display. The degree of protection varies widely. Some models must be placed three to six inches away to avoid picture degradation, while other speakers can be placed flush against a video or computer monitor without ill effects. Incidentally, I've tested a number of non-shielded monitors that didn't have any deleterious effect on video monitors.

Monitor-mounting accessories provide numerous alternatives for monitor placement. Some manufacturers offer optional mounting brackets for their speakers, while third-party suppliers provide a wide range of versatile, high-quality mounting systems. Wall-mount brackets with ball swivel joints are especially useful in the small studio environment.

THE FUTURE

What lies ahead for studio monitors? One noticeable trend is internal amplification. Once designed mainly for convenience (monitor/amp combinations have been popular with broadcast users for years), recent designs have taken the notion of the powered speaker to the next step. Models such as the Genelec 1031A, the Meyer HD-1, and the Quested Q108 incorporate state-of-the-art biamplification and active crossovers that precisely match on-

board electronics to loudspeaker components for optimum performance.

Expect to see more evolved approaches to this system, with a greater degree of electronic control over a once exclusively electro-acoustic environment. I'm still waiting for a computer-controlled system that inputs data from a hearing test of your own ears, combines it with an intelligent algorithm of your favorite mix room and/or engineer, and electronically creates the monitoring environment of your choice. ●

Powered speakers, such as Meyer Sound's HD-1 monitors, push the envelope of aural performance by combining acoustic design and active electronics.

Microphones Made Easy

IN THE WORLD OF MUSIC TECHNOL-OGY, where innovations and new products appear almost daily, the microphone hasn't changed much at all. Synthesizers, software, and effects processors are constantly updated and rendered obsolete, but when a recording engineer grabs a microphone, it's probably a model from the 1970s. Despite this apparent technological languor, the old-fashioned analog microphone remains vital to audio communication.

A microphone is a sound collector: Acoustic energy is received in the form of vibrating air particles and converted into electrical impulses. This conversion frees sound from acoustical limitations—sound waves are short-lived and travel relatively small distances before falling below the range of human hearing—and allows signals to be amplified, modulated into radio waves, and stored on various recording media.

Although Alexander Graham Bell is credited with developing the first working microphone in 1876 with his "speaking telegraph" (telephone), British physicist Sir Charles Wheatstone used the word to describe an acoustic device in 1827. Since the earliest carbon microphones (still used in most telephones), a variety of types have been developed. Of these, today's musicians generally prefer *dynamic* and *condenser* mikes.

DYNAMIC MICS

Dynamic, or *moving coil,* microphones actually are speakers that work backward. Air molecules hit a non-metallic diaphragm attached to a coil of wire that slides back and forth along a magnet (**Fig.1**). The movement of the coil produces a small electrical voltage that can be amplified through a mixer's microphone preamps and sent down the audio chain. Because its workings are relatively simple, the dynamic microphone is quite rugged. Its reliability and sound quality make it the most widely used microphone type. However, the low voltage produced by these microphones often falters through long cable (connector) runs, adding noise and distortion.

A cousin to the dynamic mic is the ribbon, or *velocity,* microphone. The ribbon mic shares certain principles with the dynamic mic, but instead of wrapping the conductor around a magnet, a thin conductive strip (the ribbon) is suspended between two magnetic poles. Ribbon microphones are extremely fragile; a poorly directed cough can shred the conductor. These microphones revolutionized broadcast audio during the 1930s by offering smooth frequency response and minimizing vocal "popping." (Bing Crosby reportedly owed his career to the ribbon, since it was the only mi-

by Neal Brighton

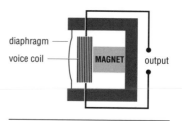

FIG. 1
In dynamic microphones, air molecules hit a diaphragm attached to a coil of wire that slides back and forth along a magnet. The movement of the coil produces a small electrical voltage.

crophone that accurately reproduced his classic croon.)

CONDENSER MICS

Unlike the electromagnetic operation of the dynamic microphone, the condenser is a purely electrical system. Separated by a small air chamber, a diaphragm and a conductive back plate are charged by an external power supply to form a capacitor (**Fig. 2**). As the diaphragm reacts to air pressure, voltage fluctuates accordingly on the back plate to produce an electrical "picture" of a sound. However, the charge that reproduces sound is tiny, so the condenser must amplify signals internally. Some condensers, such as the Neumann U87, use tube amplifiers, while others (such as the AKG 451) utilize solid-state amps. Because of the added electronics, many condensers include built-in equalization and signal-reduction pads. By increasing signal level, internal amplification also optimizes frequency response, minimizes distortion, and maintains signal integrity throughout long cable runs.

Since the condenser's diaphragm is not encumbered with the weight of a voice coil, it responds quickly to musical attacks and signal peaks. The measure of a microphone's ability to accurately reproduce these levels is called *transient response*. Condenser microphones typically exhibit better transient response than dynamic microphones, due to the condenser's smaller diaphragm mass (less mass allows quicker reactions). Condensers are expensive to manufacture and, because of their complexity, quite fragile.

WHAT ABOUT US?

Although dynamics and condensers are the most common microphone types, other designs enjoy varying degrees of popularity. *Contact* pickups usually are employed on acoustic instruments (such as acoustic guitar) and are designed to capture sound from a solid medium, rather than from the air. A member of the condenser family, the *electret* microphone utilizes a static charge and typically is powered by an internal transistor amplifier. These microphones can be made very small and often are pressed

into service in extreme close-miking situations.

Lavalier microphones, tiny elements designed to attach to clothing, enjoy wide use in television broadcasting. Another microphone with broadcast duties, the *parabolic*, is a conventional microphone linked to a reflector that focuses sound on the mic element. Sensitivity and directional characteristics are enhanced dramatically by the parabolic reflector, which is why these microphones are used at sporting events to provide "on-field" acoustics for television broadcasts.

The *piezoelectric* microphone is an early design that utilizes a flexible diaphragm and a crystal element. Sound pressure distorts the crystal, generating a corresponding voltage. Also called *crystal* or *ceramic* microphones, piezoelectrics are inexpensive and render just enough sound quality to match their low cost.

Pressure-response microphones are relative newcomers that couple a mic element to a boundary plate. The "pressure zone" principle offers good imaging quality, and the microphone can be mounted to a floor or wall. (The rock group Rush once recorded basic tracks by taping a pressure-response mic to the T-shirted chest of drummer Neil Peart.) *Shotgun* microphones are extremely directional and are favored for film location recording, where dialogue must be isolated from environmental sounds.

MIC PATTERNS

Whatever its type, the directional response, or *pickup pattern*, of a microphone can be plotted graphically to illustrate where it picks up the best sound. There are four main pattern types (**Fig. 3**).

The *cardioid* pattern resembles a small heart and is more sensitive on the front and sides of the microphone than the back. Cardioid patterns diminish sound "bleed" (where undesirable sounds are heard almost as loudly as the desired sound) when miking separate instruments in the same room. Cardioid mics are popular for vocals.

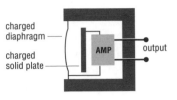

FIG. 2
Condenser microphones have an electrically charged diaphragm and conductive back plate, separated by a small air chamber to form a capacitor. As the diaphragm reacts to air pressure, voltage fluctuates on the back plate to produce an electrical "picture" of the sound.

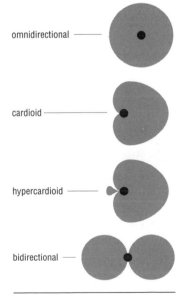

FIG. 3
The most common microphone pickup patterns.

Hypercardioid microphones are highly sensitive in front and less sensitive at the sides. This pattern diminishes the potential for feedback in live situations, since monitor speakers can be placed outside the microphone's field of sensitivity. This characteristic is called *off-axis rejection.*

A *bidirectional,* or *figure-8,* pattern is sensitive on the front and back of the microphone but not as sensitive on the sides. The bidirectional pattern is useful when recording two singers who wish to face each other while tracking a vocal.

An *omnidirectional* pattern is equally sensitive to signals from all directions.

MIC CHARACTERISTICS

An ideal microphone reproduces an acoustic input at the same signal level, no matter where the sound falls within the 20 Hz-20 kHz audio band. This is called *flat frequency response.* However, some microphones intentionally deviate from flat response to enhance live performance applications. For example, vocal microphones typically exhibit a *presence peak* in the 5-8 kHz range to help singers stand out from an instrumental mix. This characteristic is not desirable in the recording studio, where EQ decisions are the domain of the engineer.

A microphone's position in relation to the sound source also can affect frequency response. When a directional microphone is placed close to a sound source, low frequencies are boosted. This is called the *proximity effect.* (Since omnidirectional microphones pick up sound from all directions, they do not exhibit the effect.) *Off-axis coloration* is another characteristic of directional microphones: Sound from outside the microphone's optimum pattern can interfere with the desired sound source, making the overall image ill-defined or muddy.

GENERAL MIKING TIPS

Since each microphone has a distinct personality, the choice of which to use on a particular sound source is an individual one. There is no proper way to mic anything, and don't let an engineer tell you otherwise. If it sounds good, do it.

Don't forget to factor in the sound of the room. Listen for any ambient noise, strange hums, bizarre reflections, and reverberation. You may decide to pull the microphones closer to the instrument to diminish the "sound" of the environment. This is called *tight*, or *close,* miking. Be sure to bring your ear down to where the microphone is placed to get a perspective of what the microphone hears.

Vocals probably are the hardest thing to record well. The existence of so many different types of voices and vocal styles makes it impossible to use the same microphone and miking technique for everyone. Experimentation is critical. If you don't have access to any high-end vocal microphones, such as a Neumann U-87 or AKG C-414, you can still get great sounds from an inexpensive Shure SM58. Michael Hutchence of INXS once said, "Engineers always use these ridiculously expensive microphones to track my vocals and then spend hours in mixdown trying to make them sound as if they were recorded through a SM58."

EARS ARE EVERYTHING

Knowing how different microphones work helps determine which is best for a particular job. After that, it's up to your ears. While most microphones deliver optimum sound when used for the application they were designed for, never be afraid to experiment. Navigating the unknown may just deliver the sound that shakes everyone up. It's a great feeling when someone listens to your demo tape (or CD) and says, "How did you get that amazing sound?" ●

HERMAN LEONARD

The Chairman of the Board, Frank Sinatra, sings it "his way" through a Neumann U-47 tube condenser mic.

Suzanne Vega uses a Shure Beta 58 dynamic mic to help her voice fill the concert hall.

JAY BLAKESBURG

Virtual Sync: Sequencers and Tape

THE TYPICAL ELECTRONIC MUSIC STU-DIO OFTEN IS A HYBRID of "virtual" and magnetic realities; that is, sequencers producing non-tape *virtual tracks* collaborate with tape-based recorders. Recent software advances have paired digital audio with MIDI data—Opcode's *Studio Vision,* Mark of the Unicorn's *Digital Performer,* and Steinberg's *Cubase Audio* are prime examples—but the majority of sequencers still record MIDI data only and must be locked together with a tape machine to allow recording of acoustic instruments and vocals (**Fig. 1**).

For this approach to work, the tape machine and sequencer must be *synchronized* to each other. The term "synchronization" comes from the Greek word for "at the same time." For our needs, this means that the tape machine and sequencer must always start from the same precise point in time and maintain exactly the same speed as they play. This sounds like a simple requirement, but some ingenious technology is needed to successfully implement synchronization.

LOCKED UP TIGHT

For synchronization to work, one machine must follow another. MIDI Machine Control (MMC) promises to open up integrated systems where computer sequencers can control tape-recorder transport functions (see "MIDI-Controlled Recording Systems"

in this section). However, until manufacturers and software developers release more products capable of exploiting MMC, most sequencer/tape synchronization will be achieved by synching the sequencer to the tape machine.

To convey the positional information the sequencer needs, a single tape track is dedicated to recording and reproducing a *sync tone*. This audio track encodes positional information in a form that can be translated into something the sequencer can read. The reference for tape position should be established before any tracks are created, so the tone is recorded at the beginning of a session or project. (There are exceptional cases where this doesn't apply, but they are beyond the scope of most home studio productions.) A hardware sequencer or MIDI interface may provide all the facilities needed to record and read this tone (**Fig. 2**), or a third box may be required to translate the tone into a form the sequencer can understand (**Fig. 3**).

by Jeff Burger and Gary Hall

There are two basic types of sync tone: the older, variable-rate *FSK*, and the more commonly used *SMPTE* time code. Variable-rate sync drives the sequencer directly, just like a clock gear: Each tick of the "clock" is embedded in the tone and increments the sequencer by a single step of predetermined size. If the clock speeds

---

up, then the sequence speeds up, and vice versa. Unfortunately, the tempo of the sequence cannot be altered once the tone is recorded. You also must restart the sequence from its beginning every time you want to change something, because the sync tone does not contain a timing reference.

"Intelligent" or "smart" FSK solves the frustrating problem of having to start a sequence from the top by encoding MIDI *song position pointer* information into the sync tone. Using this system, the tape can be started at any point, and the sequencer "chases" to that position. However, smart FSK still doesn't allow you to change the tempo of a sequence after the sync tone is recorded.

In contrast, SMPTE time code simply records a reference to elapsed time in hours, minutes, seconds, and frames (for cueing to video). Using SMPTE gives the composer control over tempo: The tempo and starting time of the composition is specified in the sequence itself, and the sequencer is responsible for relating tempo to absolute time. SMPTE also is appropriate for situations where audio events must be related to fixed moments in time, such as cueing sound effects to film.

Early in the history of MIDI, boxes became available that recorded SMPTE time code and translated it into MIDI clocks and song position pointer messages. Because SMPTE is an absolute time reference, the translation box had to be provided with a *tempo map* to determine the start time, initial tempo, and any changes in tempo within the duration of the composition. For this reason, these "sync boxes" were elaborate, microprocessor-driven devices that were anything but simple to use.

The use of SMPTE time code in the average MIDI studio got a huge boost when the specification for *MIDI Time Code* (MTC) was ratified by the MIDI Manufacturers Association in 1987. This provided a standard way to translate SMPTE time code from tape into a form that sequencers could read directly. The result is that all of the functions of tempo mapping have been absorbed into sequencers themselves. Today, most sequencers (hardware and software) chase

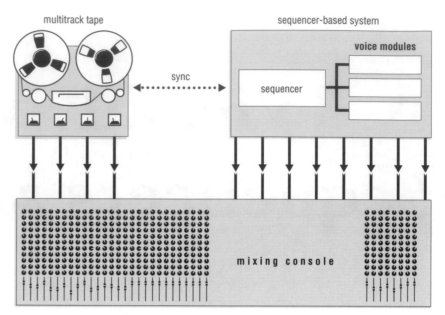

directly to MTC. (Mark of the Unicorn's *Performer* also supports the company's proprietary enhanced Direct Time Lock [DTLe], a variation of MTC.) Many hardware sequencers and MIDI interfaces are equipped to record and read SMPTE time code directly. (If you are confused about the difference between SMPTE and MTC, remember that SMPTE is the audio signal recorded onto tape, while MTC is a serial stream carried on a MIDI cable that cannot be recorded directly on tape.)

GUIDELINES FOR CLEAN SYNC

The primary objective in the synchronization process is getting a good sync tone or time code track onto tape. This process is known as *striping* the tape. If you own a modular digital multitrack, such as an Alesis ADAT or a Tascam DA-88, you don't necessarily need to use a tape track for sync. These tape-based digital recorders accept optional "add-ons" that convert their proprietary sync signals into

FIG. 1
Tape synchronization allows sequencers and multitrack decks to be combined into hybrid systems that offer the luxury of nearly unlimited virtual (sequencer-based) tracks *and* acoustically recorded vocal and instrument tracks.

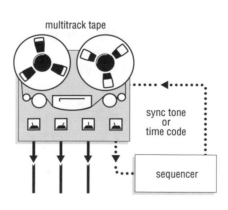

FIG. 2
Synching to tape with a sequencer that can read and write sync directly.

MTC. In other words, you've got something like a "virtual" time code track.

Analog multitrack recorders, however, must surrender a tape track to record sync. Striping an analog tape requires some care, because every type of sync tone is notoriously sensitive to tape dropout. Another source of difficulty is that the sync tracks contain large amounts of energy at the most annoying frequencies, and these have a tendency to bleed onto other tracks. To help ensure the successful striping of your tape, here are some guidelines that work for all types of sync tones.

First things first. Always stripe the tape first. It's virtually impossible to stripe a tape and find the right starting offset and tempo to match previously recorded tracks. Also, it helps to leave at least five seconds of blank tape at the beginning of the reel (or cassette). This *pre-roll* allows the mechanical tape transport time to stabilize. For the same reason, it's a good idea to maintain a few seconds of pre-roll between songs when you start recording your sequences to tape.

One thing at a time. Always record the sync tone by itself. While it might be tempting to commit a sequenced track to tape while striping, it's safer to wait. This ensures that all sequenced tracks see exactly the same signal.

Cleanliness counts. To ensure a pristine signal, always clean the heads of your tape deck before recording the sync tone. (For more information on recording session hygiene, see "Home Studio Maintenance" in this section.)

Do a complete job. In the case of SMPTE, stripe the entire tape while you make a pot of coffee. For tempo-based sync formats, you'll want to record sync on a per-song basis (for both the right tempo and a distinct point where the clock starts). In these instances, always stripe more than you need. You never know when you'll decide to tack on another chorus as you're tracking a tune, and it's better to have too much sync tone than too little.

Critical references. Always create a sequenced reference track before recording live tracks. If you wish to record live instruments before recording sequenced

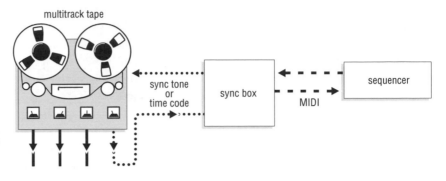

FIG. 3

Using an external conversion box, or *sync box*, to synchronize a sequencer to tape.

tracks, you'll want something to serve as a metronome. In other words, since you can't hear the sync track itself, you need to know where the beat is. In the case of time code, locking in the *starting offset* (the point in time at which the sequencer begins playing) and laying out the *tempo maps* (lists of tempo changes used by the sync box or sequencer to determine the correct song position pointers and tempos) is part of this process.

Guard tracks. To minimize the possibility of tape crosstalk interfering with the sync tone, always record the sync signal on an outside track. Most engineers put sync on the last track of a given format, such as track 8 on an 8-track deck. In addition, try to provide an empty *guard track* between the sync track and the tracks that contain your music. In our 8-track example, track 7 would remain empty. This "sonic moat" eliminates most crosstalk potential.

If there are not enough tracks to make a guard track feasible, record an instrument in the adjacent track that does not contain critical high-frequency material. (Crosstalk is most noticeable in the high frequencies.) For example, a kick-drum track can usually have some potentially troublesome highs rolled off without seriously altering its sound.

Short runs. Use the shortest lengths of high-quality connection cables possible to guard against signal dropouts and fluctuations. The more direct the signal path, the better.

Peak levels. Keep the recording level between -6 VU and 0 VU. The optimum level usually is -3 VU. However, the bottom line here is experimentation. If crosstalk is a problem on your format, strive for the lowest possible recording level that still provides good sync. If some of your tracks are to be used in other studios, a happy medium close to -3 VU helps ensure compatibility

Keeping fresh. Regenerate sync signals during transfers; generation loss has terrible effects on sync signals. If your equipment allows it, always regenerate the sync during transfers by driving your sync device from the master reel and recording the fresh output of the sync device onto the slave reel.

SYNCING WITH SMPTE

Now that you know how to record a clean signal, it's time to get your machines in sync. SMPTE time code is the chosen sync protocol for most professionals, as it allows tempo changes within a sequence and translates easily to the world of pictures. (Music videos and feature films use SMPTE as a standard reference for synching audio to visuals, whether it's matching a lip-synched performance to a master recording for MTV or cueing a sonically manipulated "big bang boom" to a fiery explosion in film post-production.) The following step-by-step instructions explain the process of recording SMPTE time code.

RECORDING TIME CODE

1. Patch the sync signal's path. For devices with their own SMPTE in/out jacks, patch directly to tape; for systems requiring converters, patch the converter's SMPTE in/out to tape and route the converter's MIDI Out to the sequencer's MIDI In. Some MIDI sequencers have a second, merged MIDI In for this purpose.

2. Set the time-code conversion device to generate time code.

3. Set the intended sync track to the optimum record level.

4. Allow at least five seconds of pre-roll (blank tape) before the point where you wish the song to begin.

5. Enable Record mode on the intended sync track and start the tape.

6. After the transport has stabilized for five seconds or more, start generating time code.

7. Stop the transport after more time code than you need has been recorded.

SMPTE PLAYBACK

To play back the recorded time code, follow these guidelines:

1. Rewind the tape to at least five seconds before the beginning of the song.

2. If you're using a stand-alone SMPTE-to-MTC converter, check to make sure that the converter's MIDI Out is connected to the sequencer's MIDI In.

3. If you intend to commit sequenced tracks to tape, patch the instruments' audio outs to the desired tape tracks and put them into Record mode.

4. Set the tempo and meter in the sequencer; program tempo maps as desired.

5. Set the time code converter to read incoming time code (if necessary).

6. Place the sequencer in External Sync mode.

7. Now, start the sequencer. The device should be waiting for a sync signal from tape.

8. Start the tape transport. The sequencer should begin playing at the beginning of the sync signal. If not, check your cables and internal/external sync settings. If there is no problem here, the problem most likely is in the record or playback level. First, try attenuating the sync playback to find the right level. If this doesn't work, go back and restripe the tape at a different level and repeat the rest of the steps until the optimum level is found.

SYNCHING TO FSK AND SMART FSK

Although SMPTE is preferable, sync tones such as FSK and Smart FSK are certainly serviceable. (Remember that you cannot change the song tempo once the sync tone is recorded.)

RECORDING SYNC TONE

1. Patch the sync signal's path. For devices with their own sync in/out jacks, patch directly to tape; for systems requiring converters, patch the converter's sync in/out to tape and route the converter's MIDI Out to the sequencer's MIDI In. Some MIDI sequencers have

a second, merged MIDI In for this purpose.

2. Set the sequencer to the desired tempo.

3. Set the sequencer (and/or converter) to Internal Sync mode.

4. Set the intended sync track to the optimum record level.

5. Set the tape at least five seconds before the point where you wish the song to begin.

6. Enable Record mode on the intended sync track and start the tape.

7. After the transport has stabilized for five seconds or more, start the sequencer. The converter should now begin generating a sync tone.

8. Stop the transport after more sync than you need has been recorded.

SYNC TONE PLAYBACK

To play back the recorded sync tone, follow these guidelines:

1. Rewind the tape to at least five seconds before the beginning of the song.

2. If you use an external converter, be sure that the converter's MIDI Out is connected to the sequencer's MIDI In.

3. If you intend to commit sequenced tracks to tape, patch the instrument's audio outs to the desired tape tracks and put the tape machine into Record mode.

4. Place the sequencer (and converter) in External Sync mode.

5. Start the sequencer. The device should be waiting for a sync signal from tape.

6. Start the tape transport. The sequencer should begin playing at the beginning of the sync signal. If not, check your cables and internal/external sync settings. If there is no problem here, the problem is most likely in the record or playback level. Try attenuating the sync playback to find the right level; if this doesn't work, restripe the tape at a different level and repeat the rest of the steps until the optimum level is found. ●

MIDI-Controlled Recording Systems

ONCE UPON A TIME, many musicians believed using MIDI and personal computers would make it easier to manage their studios and the music-making process. Instead, hours often were wasted repatching equipment, confirming proper system configurations, training an octopus to ensure the right buttons were pushed at the right time, and taking copious notes so that everything could be recreated at a later date.

But the current MIDI-controlled studio doesn't have to be a den of difficulties. Since its addition to the MIDI spec in 1992, MIDI Machine Control (MMC) has made it possible to control virtually every piece of gear in a typical MIDI studio from a single place. (MMC is a universal set of commands designed to control any type of transport—audio, video, or MIDI—from within a sequencer or controller.) By turning your independent pieces of gear into a giant meta-studio under computer control, you can turn sync problems into a distant memory, seamlessly integrate analog tape tracks with MIDI sequences, remotely control tape decks, automate your mixes, utilize the full capabilities of your signal processors, turn EQ into a dynamic extension of your sound-shaping capabilities, and make quick adjustments to a mix without worrying about rewiring or who's controlling what.

Of course, not everyone can take advantage of these capabilities, but everyone should be able to make use of certain elements. In addition, this type of structure provides a good indication of how the home studio is evolving.

Studio integration requires organization. You need to route and process MIDI data, audio signals, and machine-control code. The linchpin is your computer, which must route data between programs and between itself and the rest of the world. But before moving onto the fancy stuff, you have to deal with one of the basics: signal routing.

MIDI PATCH BAYS

The primary reason for MIDI's existence is to allow remote control of a musical instrument, typically from a second instrument or a sequencer. In other words, one device generates messages and another receives them. As soon as a MIDI studio grows to a moderate size, however, you discover situations in which you must change which devices are controlling and which are being controlled. A programmable MIDI patch bay gives you the ability to make these changes without having to unplug and replug cables.

by Chris Meyer
with Steve Oppenheimer

All devices are plugged into the patch bay (both in and out), and then routings are created and stored, either within the unit or via computer software. When I set up a studio, the first thing I do is create default data routings. Each controller, including the computer, must play every-thing. The controllers also must transfer data to and from the computer in a separate "closed loop." Once these routings are created, it's easy to switch to the one you need with a Program Change command.

If you've got several pieces of MIDI gear receiving data, whether synthesizers, MIDI-controlled mixers, or whatever, you'll probably need to run multiple discrete MIDI cables (each of which carries sixteen MIDI channels). This ensures you'll have enough channels and prevents data-clogging on the more active lines. It helps if you divide musical information (notes, etc.), transport control, mixing and signal-processing commands, and perhaps synchronization signals onto different ports or cables.

To achieve this, you'll need a multi-port MIDI interface. The best of these devices combine the functions of a MIDI patch bay/processor, computer interface, and SMPTE time code generator/reader.

AUDIO PATCH BAYS/SWITCHERS

Once MIDI data is streaming between the appropriate devices, you can turn your attention to control over routing, processing, mixing, and recording audio.

MIDI-programmable audio patch bays, like their MIDI brethren, can change routings when they receive Program Change commands. This is handy if you need to share an EQ or specialized audio enhancer and don't feel like manually repatching. It's also useful for automatically reconfiguring your effects order and routings, or switching signals that could go any number of places.

LEVEL CONTROL

Integrating the parts of your studio under computer control involves more than just routing and program changes. Your reach can extend to controlling audio levels, too. Fortunately, most MIDI instruments allow you to control output level via Continuous Controller 7 (Master Volume). Many also allow panning with Controller 10 and setting the balance between two layered sounds with Controller 8.

But controlling instrument output levels via Controller 7 can disrupt your gain structure, adding noise to the audio chain. In setting up your mixer, you adjust levels at various points to optimize the signal-to-noise ratio. To maintain clean sound, you need to keep input levels relatively constant and adjust mix levels with the faders. If you change levels at the instrument outputs with MIDI, the mixer receives fluctuating input levels, and your painstakingly constructed gain structure goes out the window. In addition, your instruments may not have smooth MIDI Volume control (listen for zippering or glitching). Besides, instrument outputs aren't the only audio levels that need to be controlled.

One answer is MIDI-controlled VCA boxes, which can vary the level of any audio signal passing through them. You can use these devices on MIDI instruments or non-MIDI sources. By adding the VCA box at the mixer's insert points, you can automate level changes after the mixer's critical gain stages; adding VCAs at the mixer channel direct outs can control track levels going to multitrack without affecting the console's gain structure. You also can use a VCA box to control the levels of your tape tracks.

MIDI MIXERS

You'll need to mix the audio at some point, too. If you take the modular approach, where everything goes through MIDI-controlled processors and a VCA box, all you need is a multiple-input line mixer and a good headphone amp for monitoring. But for complete studio automation, your best choice might be a MIDI-controlled mixer that places level, panning, EQ, and effects sends under computer command.

MIDI-controllable mixers integrate multiple functions. One of the earliest and most ambitious attempts was Yamaha's DMP7. This 8 x 2 digital mixer offers three onboard signal processors, complete MIDI control, and motorized faders that constantly show the current parameter values. The original $4,000 price tag chilled its reception among semi-professionals, but many are still in use.

A MIDI patch bay lets you route signals between all connected MIDI devices in your studio.

Signal Processors

As with synthesizers, most modern signal processors respond to MIDI Program Changes and controllers. Applications can be as simple as remotely changing the wet/dry mix or as radical as timing a reverb's gate to drum hits.

Equalization provides a more subtle (and underused) method for altering timbres. Roland, Rane, Yamaha, DigiTech, Peavey, and Akai (to name a few) make, or have made, programmable equalizers that respond to MIDI Program Changes. Some allow individual bands to be dynamically changed using MIDI controllers, either for remote-control tweaking or for a musical effect in the middle of a song.

Another useful signal-processing beast you can tame via MIDI is the MIDI-controlled preamp. Most folks probably consider these strictly guitar gadgets, but they can provide timbral flexibility and muscle for many applications. As with MIDI instruments, MIDI-controlled preamps, effects, and EQs usually can download and save their patches via SysEx.

The Sequencer

In many MIDI studios, the sequencer is the heart of the enterprise. It's where you store not only the note data, but the controller data, program changes, and MMC machine instructions.

When shopping for a sequencer, select a program that lets you look at multiple MIDI ports and has onscreen "faders" and graphic controller editing. Although I prefer using a hardware fader box, it's nice to see software counterparts onscreen for reference. Graphic controller editing is important for easily checking out information already recorded. Build up some fader palettes dedicated to various functions: one for the main volume of all your instruments, one for dynamic control of parameters in your multi-effects, and one to control your programmable EQs. It's also useful to have onscreen sliders or other controls for changing programs on all your devices.

Incidentally, when controlling tape-track levels within a sequencer, don't split them off on a separate virtual-fader palette; you'll confuse the issue by thinking too much about where the physical control is happening. Just think about the

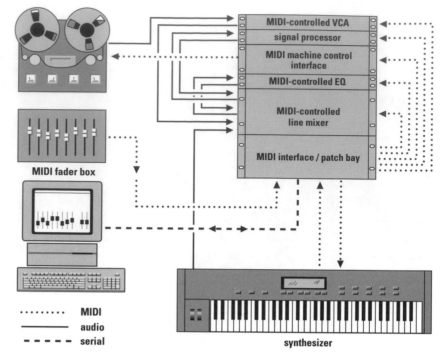

onscreen faders as the means for adjusting levels, and hopefully you'll forget (after initial setup) exactly where that level change is taking place. The same goes for controlling EQ and effects, whether onboard an instrument or in a rack. From your control station, it should all be one meta-studio to you.

Pick a sequencer and tape recorder that speaks MMC. In addition to integrating the recording process, this leaves the door open for expanding the number of tracks in your studio. A few sequencers, mostly on the Mac, have hard-disk recording integrated into them, and several Mac and PC systems address digital audio and sample playback cards inside the computer as if they were merely components of your MIDI system.

More MMC sequencer support is coming; don't underestimate the power of combining a few tracks of random-access digital audio under sequencer control with several linear tracks on an MMC-capable tape machine, such as the Alesis ADAT or Tascam DA-88 digital multitrack recorders.

Software Utilities

To streamline control of your environment, try adding a number of utilities directly to your computer. Since I'm a Macintosh user, I'll focus on that environment. Every power-user by now has

A hypothetical mixerless MIDI-controlled studio system. The computer-based sequencer stores information generated by the synth and MIDI fader box and sends the appropriate control signals to the tape deck, VCA box, programmable EQ, programmable DSP box, and MIDI-controlled line mixer.

adopted some form of "macro" program that will perform complex actions in response to a single keystroke. Some use voice-recognition systems such as Articulate Systems' Voice Navigator for hands-off operation. Programs and operating-system extensions such as the *HyperMIDI/HyperCard* duo and UserLand's *Frontier* for the Macintosh allow you to write your own programs and control the linkages between them.

Adventurous Macintosh users should consider Opcode's *MAX*. Besides allowing you to write custom MIDI applications, this iconic programming environment includes hooks to let you control a *QuickTime* movie or a CD-ROM player. It even accepts input from a Mattel/Nintendo Power Glove by way of Transfinite's Gold Brick Nintendo-to-ADB adapter. I've used *MAX* to create my own software controllers and translators.

If you want custom MIDI processing but don't need the low-level control of *MAX*, Dr. T's *Interactor,* a similar iconic programming language for the Macintosh, could be a good choice. Many *Interactor* patches already are set up for higher-level MIDI functions, so it's easier to learn than *MAX*.

SOFTWARE INTEGRATION

Another part of integrating your hardware is routing data to, from, and between computer programs. Routing data within the computer—Interapplication Communication, or IAC—makes it possible to, say, route sequencer data to trigger sounds played back by a computer sound chip or card, or let multiple programs, such as a sequencer and media integration program playing digital audio files, share the same internal time base.

Macintosh users have had this capability for a while. Apple's *MIDI Manager* system extension presents an onscreen "patch bay" that lets you interconnect every compatible MIDI program that is running. You just click-and-drag virtual "wires" between the programs' onscreen input and output ports.

PC users don't have a system-level utility for IAC, but *Windows 3.1* offers a standardized MIDI driver protocol which, if expanded upon, could offer functionality similar to *MIDI Manager*. The *MIDI*

Mapper utility included with version 3.1 is a specialized driver that maps MIDI Program Changes to a General MIDI set and relieves programs of having to worry about which type of MIDI interface is installed, but it does not perform IAC.

On the Atari, Steinberg's *M.ROS* and Dr. T's *MPE* offer capabilities somewhat similar to *MIDI Manager* for programs written specifically for those environments. The Amiga has built-in multitasking, and by utilizing *ARexx* or writing a bit of extra code, Amiga programmers can allow multiple MIDI programs to share the serial ports and interchange data. *MPE* also operates in the Amiga environment.

One step beyond IAC systems such as *MIDI Manager* is Opcode's *Open Music System (OMS)*. This Macintosh program extends the reach of the computer by allowing you to name all MIDI devices in your studio and identify the MIDI port and channel where each is located. An *OMS*-compatible program uses this information to route data to the appropriate devices. This may entail sending a Program Change message to your MIDI patch bay, or perhaps addressing a specific port of a multi-port MIDI interface.

HARDWARE CONTROLLERS

At this point, you have MIDI devices interconnected to automatically route and process MIDI and audio data, and control instrument parameters and patches, audio

The lean approach to a MIDI-controlled system can be achieved with a MIDI fader controller, a programmable MIDI mixer, and two preset MIDI-controlled effects processors.

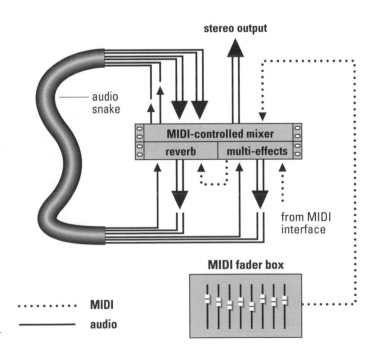

levels, EQ, effects, mixing, and tape transports. Your computer programs are cooperatively processing, sharing, and distributing the MIDI data. But you still need to control these various parts with a computer user interface.

Although pointing devices such as mice and trackballs are a big improvement over the four cursor keys found on most computer keyboards, they are not always the best control-input options. It's hard to perform a mix by grabbing one onscreen slider at a time with a mouse, or to quickly shuttle transport controls by moving an arrow swiftly across the screen and clicking. You may want to add some extra hardware to get a better grip on your newly integrated studio.

A growing number of MIDI hardware controllers are available. On the simple side, several companies make remote MIDI program changers and footswitch controllers, some of which can send a respectable packet of MIDI messages at the stomp of a foot. There are also numerous MIDI fader boxes available that allow you to assign any MIDI message to a set of hardware sliders.

Aside from button, fader, and knob controllers, plenty of creative user interface possibilities are developing. For instance, the aforementioned Mattel/Nintendo Power Glove and Don Buchla's Lightning permit gestural input. There also are many commercial MIDI instrument and pad controllers, such as Buchla's Thunder or KAT's drumKAT, that can be creatively adapted to a variety of MIDI control functions.

CONCLUSION

Of course, software developments continue and the increasing importance of multimedia indicates a long life for the integrated system concept. Programs

such as Passport Designs' *Producer*—which coordinates multiple tracks of MIDI sequences, 8- and 16-bit digital audio, *QuickTime* movies, and VCRs compatible with Sony's VISCA protocol—will probably become more popular and

A MIDI fader box lets you generate continuous controller messages which can automate many aspects of your MIDI studio.

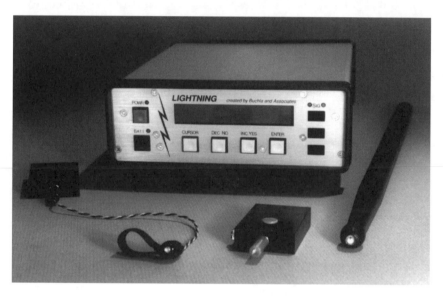

more powerful. Even more significant is the support computer companies are giving MIDI in their multimedia plans. Plainly, integrated systems are the future of the recording studio.   ●

Buchla's Lightning is a gestural MIDI controller that generates messages based on movements of the controller wands in space.

Home Studio Maintenance

AFTER COLLECTING THOUSANDS OF DOLLARS WORTH OF EQUIPMENT, you'd think musicians would protect their investments. Ha! The average home studio is a shameless den of neglect. I've visited countless personal (and sadly, some professional) studios where poor maintenance crippled the equipment's sound quality and accelerated major overhauls.

But a little foresight can change everything. In professional studios, where equipment often runs around the clock, preventative maintenance schedules ensure that every session runs as smoothly as possible. These "clean routines" are not difficult, and home recordists who spend a few minutes playing audio domestic (maid and butler uniforms are optional) reap the benefits of improved system quality and longevity.

THE CLEAN SCHEME

If more musicians took the following advice, this statement would overstate the obvious: Keeping equipment clean prevents breakdowns. Dirt and electrical equipment are sworn enemies, so cover mixing consoles, multitrack decks, keyboards, etc. with pieces of non-porous material (vinyl, plastic, etc.) to prevent dust invasions.

Musicians who use their studio daily and can't be bothered with the constant covering/uncovering of equipment should "clean house" every two weeks: Simply spray Windex (or a similar non-abrasive cleaner) onto a cloth and wipe down all equipment surfaces. Do *not* spray the cleaner directly onto your gear. Employ an old-fashioned feather duster to gently lift dust from the tiny surface areas between knobs, sliders, and faders.

TAPE-DECK SANITATION

As recording tape runs along the drive mechanisms of an analog deck, magnetic oxide particles are knocked off. If the particles scatter after running across the record head, they often become magnetized and can cause serious problems. In one case, a client who never cleaned his multitrack deck was plagued by frequent tape dropouts. I discovered that an oxide buildup on the pinch roller was "unrecording" certain tracks as the tape ran past.

Oxide deposits also can carve gorges into your record and playback heads. A moving tape that picks up stray particles scratches the heads like fine sandpaper. And believe me, it doesn't take centuries to etch your heads away. While head wear is inevitable, the process can be slowed considerably by making your deck a particle-free zone.

by Neal Brighton

The process of cleaning heads is the same for multitracks, 2-track reel-to-reel decks, and cassette recorders. Alcohol

(100 percent pure) is the cleaning solution of choice for metal parts, because it cleans and then evaporates. Alcohol is not recommended for use on rubber parts; it can dry them out and cause surface cracking. However, specialized solutions are available that can safely clean rubber *and* metal parts.

Using a good-quality cotton swab, dip into your cleaning solution and wipe down the front and side surfaces of the heads (**Fig. 1**). Then clean the tape guides and idler arms. Check for debris hiding on the top and bottom lips of the tape guides. Next, clean the pinch roller (remember, don't use alcohol), and don't stop scrubbing until all of the oxide particles, which appear as brown residue, are "terminated." Finally, hit the plastic capstan with a few wipes of a clean, damp cloth.

DEMAGNETIZING

Once you've cleaned up, you have another important task: demagnetizing the heads, tape guides, and idler arms. Obviously, if any of these metal parts are magnetized, they could erase your master tape (and possibly, your masterpiece). Compact demagnetizers (**Fig. 2**), which can be purchased at most electrical supply shops, are invaluable for ensuring high audio quality and are great for preventative maintenance.

Demagnetizing is easy, but *do not* turn on the tape deck during the procedure. An accidental magnetic field fed into "powered up" heads can damage the tape recorder's internal amplifiers. Also, it should be obvious that any master tape lying near (or on) the tape deck during demagnetization could be subject to erasure.

Turn on the demagnetizer an arm's length from your deck, then slowly bring the rubber tip of the demagnetizer towards the right idler arm. Then, working right to left, slowly pass the demagnetizer over each metal part of the tape drive mechanism, as shown in **Fig. 3**. (Reverse the procedure if you're left-handed.) Upon completion, draw the demagnetizer back at least an arm's length away from the deck before turning it off. If the demagnetizer is switched off too soon, it will dump the newly collected debris back onto the tape deck.

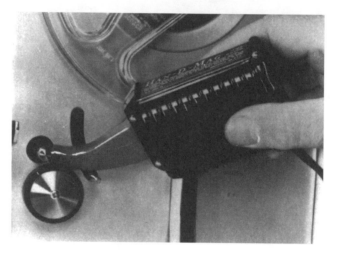

PETER DIGGS

Get into the habit of cleaning and demagnetizing your decks before each use. In addition, clean the tape heads and tape guards after every four hours of use. Repeated cleanings are especially important when using fresh tape, because new tape (and very old tape) sheds more oxide.

DAT DETAILING

The maintenance of analog decks—whether a professional multitrack or cassette ministudio—is pretty much the same. DAT recorders are another story. The inner workings of a DAT deck are closer to those of a video recorder. The rotary head spins at a high speed, and the DAT tape must be pulled from its casing and wrapped around the head.

Because DAT recorders store digital information on an analog medium (magnetic tape), it's important to keep the heads clean to prevent tape dropouts. If dirt causes the DAT to misread data—so

FIG. 1 (top)
Cleaning the playback head on a Tascam MS-16 16-track recorder.

FIG. 2 (bottom)
Hand-held demagnetizers allow easy access to a recorder's metal parts.

much that error correction is hopelessly embattled—it won't be beautiful music that reaches the signal outputs.

Consumer DAT head cleaners are available and easy to use (just pop in the cassette and push Play), but usually aren't thorough enough to remove the grime produced by heavy studio use. The preferred cleaning method is to manually scrub the head with a long-handled foam swab and any reputable video head-cleaning solution. Cotton swabs are dangerous, because loose fibers can attach to the head and cause dropouts.

Open the top panel of the DAT deck (**Fig. 4**) and keep a flashlight handy for spot illumination. Just as in the procedure for analog recorders, clean the tape guides *and* the heads. Be sure to let the deck stand open for ten minutes to allow ventilation and drying of the cleaning solution.

MIXER MAINTENANCE

Keeping your mixer free of dust and dirt is critical, because noisy pots and faders can produce noisy master tapes. Use a damp cloth to clean the dust from the board's surfaces, and wipe away the grease pencil marks that indicated fader levels during previous mixes. Be careful not to let dust or grease pencil debris fall into the fader slots. Usually, the primary reason for noisy faders is all the human hair, dirt, and lunch crumbs that drop between the channel paths and faders. (Only those who enjoy dancing with tragedy should eat over their mixer.)

To check if your faders are "slimed," run a pure 1 kHz tone through each input module. While the tone is sounding, slide the fader up and down. Listen for crackles and pops. Be sure to do this test with a pure tone, as a conventional music program may disguise noises.

If you hear pops and crackles, a commercial contact cleaner (such as Blue Shield or Cramolin) should restore silence. However, don't just squirt the cleaner blindly into the fader. When you hear a noise, mark the fader level with a grease pencil. Then peek inside the fader slot to determine if the circuit board is mounted to the right, left, or bottom of the input module. You must direct the contact cleaner towards the contacts of the circuit board to effect any improvement. Next, turn off the tone and slide the fader up and down a few times. Do a final check with the tone generator to make sure the fader is noiseless. If not, repeat the process. It may take a few squirts to completely clean the fader.

Sometimes hairs or crumbs attach themselves to the metal fader guide, and a blast of compressed air is needed to clear the obstruction (**Fig. 5**). Cans of compressed air usually are available at electronics stores. Make sure the nozzle can fit into small places and that the

FIG. 3
Demagnetizing heads and metal tape guides helps ensure that oxide gremlins won't mess with your master tapes.

PETER DIGGS

◉ The Basic Toolkit

Boy Scouts and recording engineers know the value of being prepared. Technology is fickle, and sometimes sessions are plagued by equipment malfunctions. Often, the demon is something simple that can be cured with a trip to the trusty toolbox. You don't need to be a qualified repair tech to undertake the basic maintenance tips outlined in this chapter, but you do need the following items:

1. A set of small- and medium-size screwdrivers, flat and Phillips heads
2. Wire cutters
3. Small and medium-size needle-nose pliers
4. A tone generator (if your board does not have one) with 100 Hz, 1 kHz, and 10 kHz settings
5. Glass cleaner
6. A soft, clean rag (or paper towels)
7. Cleaning alcohol
8. Rubber cleaner
9. A demagnetizer
10. An ohmmeter
11. An assortment of cotton and foam swabs
12. A can of compressed air (make sure propellant is safe for electronic use)
13. Red masking tape
14. A soldering iron and solder

chemical propellant is safe for use with electronic equipment.

Now use the 1 kHz tone to systematically check your board input by input. Listen carefully for scratchy pan pots, aux sends, mute buttons, etc., and then make a list of all problem components.

While it may not be practical (or within your skills) to replace these parts yourself, it's a good practice to map out your console's "problem geography." For instance, if input five has a scratchy pan pot, you'll know to avoid it when returning a track that requires panning changes during mixdown. If you find a large number of bad pots, call a knowledgeable technician and get them replaced. Don't be lazy; any audible cracks and pops *will* become part of your finished mixes.

GETTING ALIGNED

Proper alignment of your tape deck is another important maintenance procedure, and one that few home recordists either understand or practice. Unfortunately, describing a complete alignment procedure would encompass an entire article (and it's not exactly a thrilling read). Instead, here's a quick test that can determine what shape your deck is in.

First, disable any noise reduction (dbx or Dolby) and record 30 seconds of a 1 kHz tone at "0" VU. Be sure to use Input (or Record) mode. Repeat the procedure with 10 kHz and 100 Hz tones. Then rewind the tape and put your deck into Repro (or Play) mode. If your deck is properly aligned, all three tones will replay at 0 VU, which is the same level you recorded them. Don't panic if 10 kHz is a little off; semi-pro decks often have a looser tolerance at higher frequencies. However, if all the tones come back completely out of whack, you should call in a technician to align your deck. If you want pristine masters, it's worth the expense.

TAPE TENDERNESS

Remember that the care and maintenance of your master tapes is as important as the care you give your equipment. Tape-based masters can last many years, *if* you take the time to store them properly.

Spool off important reel-to-reel masters at normal play speed (or slow rewind, if available) so your hit songs aren't inadvertently shredded by a demonic full-speed rewind. Store all of your tapes "tails out" (backwards) to prevent print-through (ghostly audio images that appear when unstable magnetic bits start vacationing at other tape locations), and secure down the end of the master with splicing tape. Also, you should label the boxes with the names of the songs, tape speed, type of noise reduction, recording date, artist, etc. Believe me, every bit of information comes in handy at one time

PETER DIGGS

FIG. 4
A long-handled foam swab is recommended for cleaning a DAT recorder's rotary head. The same process can be used to clean the mechanisms on the Alesis ADAT (S-VHS) and the Tascam DA-88 (8 mm).

⦿ More Maintenance Tips

• **I**f your studio is in constant use, it's advisable to leave your mixer and power amp(s) on. When AC power is switched on, a spike occurs before the power settles down to its normal voltage. While most equipment deals with these spikes just fine, years of constant ons and offs can damage power supplies.

• Feedback loops are common in studio environments, and it only takes one mistake to turn an expensive speaker into stir-fry. If you want to protect your monitor speakers, put fuses on them. In-line fuses can be purchased at your local electronics store. Start with a fast-blow one-amp fuse hooked onto the positive side of your speaker. Find a comfortable monitoring level and then increase the volume to see where the fuse blows. The higher the amperage of the fuse, the higher the volume it allows before self-destructing. Obviously, the fuse should blow long before the speaker shreds.

• To prevent surprises during important sessions, have an ohmmeter available to test cables for shorts. Be sure to label bad cables with red tape, so they don't get thrown back into the "good" pile. In addition, keep some assorted connectors and adapters on hand for cable repairs.

• Knowing the ins and outs of your mixing console is critical during troubleshooting, so keep a signal-flow chart handy. Trying to trace mixer problems without this valuable document is like cruising the Los Angeles freeway system without a map.

or another. Lastly, never stack tapes on top of each other (stand them up like toy soldiers), and always make sure the storage area is cool and dry.

Multitrack and stereo master cassettes, DAT masters, S-VHS tapes (Alesis ADAT format), and 8 mm tapes (Tascam DA-88 format) never should be stored without being completely rewound. The plastic casing can protect the tape inside to a point, but don't tempt fate by leaving cassettes outside of their storage boxes or sleeves. Ideal storage environments are the same as for reel-to-reel masters: cool and dry.

MINIMAL DOWNTIME

Good working habits and a bi-monthly routine of preventative maintenance can help your equipment deliver optimum performance. Knowing when you really *do* need a professional technician, and when you'd simply be wasting his or her

PETER DIGGS

time (and your money), is not an insignificant reward for delving into the maintenance mindset. And even more importantly, an ounce of preventative maintenance can be worth a pound of your money. ●

FIG. 5
A blast of compressed air can clean up grungy fader guides.

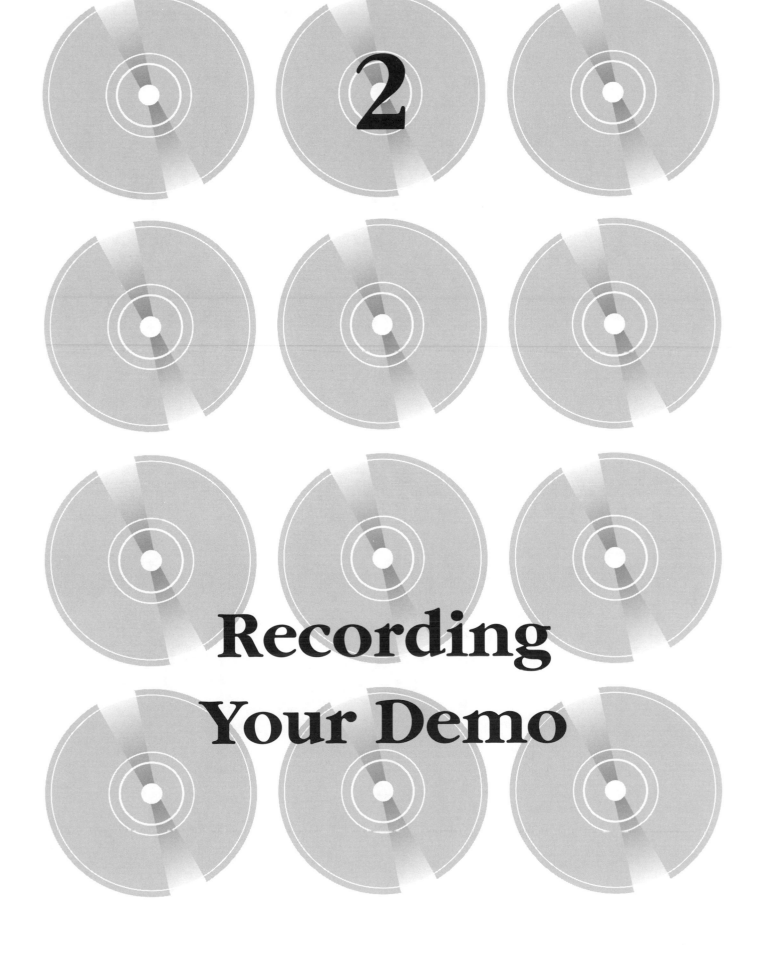

2

Recording
Your Demo

Ultimate Drum Tracks

POOR RINGO. During the early years of Beatlemania, the legendary drummer was recorded with one mic on his kick drum and one mic hanging over his head. Two microphones captured the beat that drove the band that changed rock 'n' roll. Today, some engineers use two mics just to record a snare drum. Was Ringo robbed?

Hardly. The Beatles' primary recording engineers, Norman Smith and Geoff Emerick, had the ears and imagination to wring one hell of a boom-boom-snap from two microphones. And although the current style of slaughterhouse snares (often mixed louder than the lead vocal) was undeveloped in the 1960s, Ringo's drums still rock the house.

Home and project studio owners should be inspired by the fact that the limitations of early pop recording didn't prevent Smith and Emerick from laying down a timeless thump. Good ears, decent microphones, and a little bit of forethought empower virtually anyone to record crushing drum tracks.

PREPPING THE DRUM KIT

Drums can take forever to record, because even basic kits contain a jungle of hardware that creaks, rattles, and moans. Microphones record every sonic blemish, so pristine drum tracking requires taming mechanical noises.

When the drums are set up, check the kit for loose connections. If cymbal or tom stands rattle, wrap some foam around noisy joints and tape everything down with heavy-duty vent tape. Whining kick-drum pedals may be silenced by spraying the moving parts with a lubricant such as WD-40.

Once everything is battened down, have the drummer play a simple beat, occasionally throwing in tom-tom fills and cymbal crashes. If everything sounds great, buy a lottery ticket immediately, because you're blessed with incredible luck. Most likely, you'll hear a symphony of obnoxious drum overtones, a paper-thin snare, and more squeaks and rattles.

At this point, it's senseless to drive yourself crazy tracing minute problems. Go for the big ones. Find the new rattles exposed by the drummer's performance and tape them down. If overtones are excessive, have the drummer retune the offending drums until they produce a clean, full-bodied sound. Be prepared to jump in and help, because many drummers are clueless about timbre. (I've never regretted paying a renowned session drummer to teach me how to tune drums.)

by Michael Molenda

If tuning and retuning won't kill the offensive overtones, place two fingers on the drum head, approximately one-half inch from the hardware rim, and move them in a circle around the head until you find a position where the overtones are muted. Now cover the "hot spot" with a single piece of vent tape. Although this is an over-simplified remedy, the tape should muffle the overtone ring. Some drummers use commercial "ring killers," homemade muting templates cut from old drum heads, and even feminine hygiene napkins to diminish these overtones.

Be careful not to use so much tape that the drum begins to sound like a telephone book when struck (unless, of course, that's the sound you want). However, in even the best cases, muting overtones compromises the natural tonality of the drum. If the ring cannot be tuned out of the drum and you must resort to taping heads, be prepared to make some concessions between the overtones and "pure tone."

There's a reason for all this toil and trouble: Drum kits that sound great acoustically usually retain that quality under the bitter scrutiny of microphones. You'll appreciate the energy spent hunting down noises and overtones when it's time to mic individual drums.

THE SNARE DRUM

Recording an absolutely slamming snare sound is the best way to get a nervous producer and/or band off your back. I read about this trick years ago in an interview with master engineer Tom Lord-Alge, and it has never failed me. (Thank you, Tom!) It's somewhat puzzling *why* a meaty snare engenders trust, considering that a good recording is composed of much more than a thwack. But don't waste time pondering psychology when you could be testing mic positions.

The classic snare miking technique involves positioning a dynamic mic an inch or two over the snare rim opposite the drummer and an inch above the top drum head. My favorite snare mic is a Shure SM57, because it records the impact of stick to drum without accentuating overtones. Your style may favor broader timbres, so be sure to experiment with different microphones.

Some engineers also mic the bottom head to capture the rattle of the snare springs. You can use another dynamic mic for this position, or even experiment with a condenser. (Be sure to pad the

mic input at least -10 dB to avoid frying the condenser's diaphragm with massive sound pressure levels.) I'm not a huge fan of this method, as more mics means more sound leakage from the kick drum, cymbals, and toms. Also, few drummers maintain their snare assemblies in top form, so bottom miking often reproduces sonic anomalies (creaks, buzzes, etc.) along with the increased snare thwack. This doesn't mean you should abandon experimentation, but be sure to listen very critically every time you audition different mic positions.

SNARE TRICKS

In modern music, an isolated snare treated with an individual reverb (or even mixed "dry") enhances sonic impact. Unfortunately, getting a live snare sound without cymbals and toms bleeding into the mic is problematic. Noise gating to tape is risky, because the high input threshold required to shut out cymbal crashes can clip the snare signal if the drummer drops the intensity of his or her strokes.

An expander is a more practical tool. Simply put, expansion diminishes the level of signals under a user-set threshold. What makes this device perfect for drums is that it treats signals more gently than the brusque on/off action of a noise gate. To a noise gate, a loud cymbal crash is a loud cymbal crash. Depending on the predetermined signal threshold, the gate either shuts down the crash or lets it through. If the drummer smacks a cymbal harder than expected, the gate opens and a painfully loud sizzle bleeds into the snare mic.

From his technique to his drum kit, Mr. Ringo Starr (far left, with legendary fab friends) is the epitome of simplicity, and yet he rocks as hard as any drummer who has embraced the pop idiom. I always love it when a drummer brings a "Ringo kit" (kick, snare, rack tom, floor tom, hi-hat, two crash cymbals, and a ride cymbal) into the studio. Sparse kits are easy to mike, and if the tuning is good, the sound can be incredible.

Because an expander "quiets down" unwanted signals, cymbal explosions and tom fills are not catastrophic. When the expansion threshold is set to cut signals below the level of the snare hits, the kick drum, cymbals, and toms appear discreetly in the background. During mixdown, when expansion already has recorded snare levels much hotter than peripheral sounds, careful noise gating can complete sonic isolation.

THE KICK DRUM

Rap music has thrown down the gauntlet regarding kick drum sounds. Today, anyone recording acoustic drums must acknowledge the sonic power of heavily processed electronic percussion. This doesn't mean that the kick drum on a folk-rock ballad should blow the doors off a Volvo, only that maximum impact is preeminent.

Really getting down with a kick drum requires a large-diaphragm dynamic mic, such as an AKG D12E, an Electro-Voice RE20, or a Sennheiser MD 421. For pop sounds, convince the drummer to remove his or her front drum head. (Double-headed drums add overtones that usually are appropriate only for jazz.) Some drummers cut a hole in the front head to facilitate miking, and this often makes a "best of both worlds" situation possible. However, even these modified front heads can produce flabby overtones. Listen carefully to ensure the kick sound is uncompromised. For example, a hole with a sloppy, jagged cut sometimes can produce noticeable creaks.

Pushing a foam pad or blanket against the rear head minimizes rings and improves the thud factor. Moving the mic closer to the drum head adds more thump (the mic is closer to the beater), while moving it away records more overtones. For snappy pop kicks, I usually position the mic approximately five inches inside the drum and tilt it slightly towards the floor tom. This position records a clear, tight kick (the minute off-axis position avoids the "woofs" caused by air exploding directly into the mic) with a robust low end.

If a drummer refuses to remove a solid front head (with no mic hole), or if you want to experiment with true double-headed sounds, try to use the accentuated overtones to good advantage. In these instances, good tuning is essential, so spend the time to get the drums sounding right. Diminish any high-end ringing and tune the fundamental overtone to a timbre that complements the low end of the kick. My favorite double-headed kick sound was recorded by placing an AKG C414 condenser mic two feet in front of the kick drum, pointed dead center at the exterior head. The mic was padded -20 dB to ensure the sonic impact didn't shred the diaphragm. This combination of mic type and positioning produced immense, booming kicks that sounded like dinosaur stomps.

KICK TRICKS

If you *do* want to blow the doors off a Volvo, even more intense kicks can be

ROGER RESSMEYER

recorded by compressing the signal -10 dB at a ratio of 2:1, boosting the EQ at 100 Hz, and then running it through a noise gate to shut down the boom a few milliseconds after the initial impact. I've blown a few speaker fuses this way, but what a punch!

Less catastrophic kicks are produced by diminishing extraneous snare, tom, and cymbal sounds with an expander. This procedure allows the kick drum to be the loudest sound recorded on tape, an obvious advantage if you desire a pounding track. Further isolation can be gained by draping a heavy blanket over the kick drum and microphone to make a "sound tent."

A "musical" drumming style can offer big career payoffs; just look at Narada Michael Walden. His sensitivity to song structures led him from the drum throne to the producer's desk. Some critics shudder at Walden's pristine, calculated production for mega-hit divas Whitney Houston and Mariah Carey, but there is no lack of passion in the drum tracks he laid down for the Mahavishnu Orchestra and Jeff Beck.

TOMS

Tom fills add spice to a track. Much of their power depends on the creativity of the drummer, but it certainly doesn't hurt if you make each drum sound like a cannon. Shure SM57s often are used in live performance miking, and serve admirably in the budget studio. However, you can record bigger booms with a Sennheiser MD 421 or similar model that hears more low end.

Place the microphone approximately two to four inches over the top drum head, listening critically for a harmonious blend of drum tone and percussive impact. To achieve maximum tonal control and articulation, try to mike each tom individually. However, if you don't have enough microphones or channel inputs on your mixer, you can use one mic to record the rack toms and another to record the floor tom (or toms). Position the rack-tom mic in the middle of the tom setup, approximately four inches above the top rims and one foot back. The floor-tom mic should be placed closer, approximately two inches above the outside rim of the head. (If the drummer uses two or more floor toms, try to position the mic in the middle of the drums and no more than four inches above the top heads.)

To intensify the sonic impact of the toms, I often compress the drums to tape while recording. I assign the individual tom tracks to a left/right subgroup and use a dual (stereo) compressor to process the submix. The processed "tom" submix is recorded to tape on two separate tracks to maintain stereo imaging. Subtle compression settings usually work the best, as severe compression can cause any cymbal hits that leak into the tom mics to sound like high-end splatters. During mixdown, I typically run the tom submix through a stereo expander to wipe out snare and cymbal bleed. Remember, the cleaner the tom tracks, the more they'll punch out of the mix during drum fills.

HI-HATS

Since the hi-hat often is the linear time-keeper in popular music, it's important that it be crisp and articulate. I usually use a small diaphragm condenser mic,

such as one of AKG's Blue Line series, positioned three inches from the top hi-hat at a 45-degree angle. It helps to cut the bass frequencies while recording so that kick drum and tom sounds are de-

STEVE JENNINGS

emphasized. Moving the mic a few feet away from the hi-hat provides a hi-hat/cymbal perspective that can be used instead of an overhead mic if you're short on microphones or mixer inputs.

OVERHEADS

Overhead mics record more than just cymbal crashes; they document the spatial characteristics of a drummer's personal kit configuration. This perspective is as important to the drummer as a guitar/amp marriage is to the guitarist.

One of the classic overhead positions consists of two condenser mics on boom stands, placed about three to five feet over the drummer's head. A left-side mic is pointed at the left-side cymbals, and a right-side mic is aimed at the right-side cymbals. A variation, often called the "X" position, requires moving the boom stands close together over the drummer's head and pointing the left mic towards the right cymbals and vice versa.

A subtle alteration of the X pattern involves lowering the mics until they rest behind the drummer's ears (**Fig. 1**). I've found that this position enhances the organic sound of the drums and provides an interesting "drummer's perspective" of the stereo field. Even though the mics are lower, cymbal crispness is uncompro-

Neil Peart, drummer for progressive rock icon Rush, has a virtual city of drums at his disposal. How would the typical home or project studio recordist deal with such an immense kit? One option is to set up individual mics for the kick drum and snare, then use two overhead mics to record the multitude of toms and cymbals.

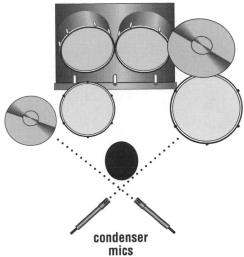

condenser mics

mised. An added benefit is that toms appear quite robust in the overheads, often making it unnecessary to EQ the individual tom tracks. (Remember, less processing equals cleaner tracks.)

Want to join the "Back to Mono" movement of legendary producer Phil Spector? Position a condenser mic—I use an AKG C414—approximately ten feet in front of the drums at the drummer's chest level (**Fig. 2**). This position records the entire drum kit and sounds great when blended with the individual drum tracks. I've often used this position as my sole "overhead" mic when tracks are limited. I simply pan the kick and snare to center, then place the hi-hat to the right and the mono room mic to the left.

A DRUM ROLL, PLEASE

Drums are such an integral component of rock music that scores of anecdotes exist regarding bizarre recording techniques.

Elvis' drummer, J.D. Fontana, once remarked that he cut many classic tracks by slapping cardboard boxes. New wave godfather Nick Lowe expressed an affinity for the "telephone book" snare. And, according to a Dick Clark biography, when the drums were too loud during the session for "The Monster Mash," the engineers simply moved the kit away from *the* microphone and draped blankets over the toms, kick, and snare. (Yep, back in the old days, vocals and instruments sometimes were recorded through a single microphone!)

Once again, practical examples prove that there is no "right" or "wrong" way to

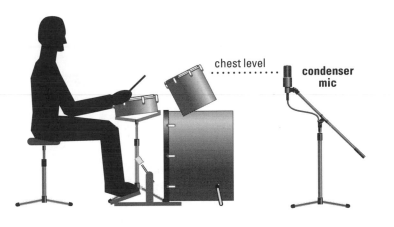

chest level .... **condenser mic**

record a drum kit. The key issue of drum tracking is to do whatever it takes to drive the song. If you keep your creative options open, you'll find that most limitations are merely challenges. After all, if you can't get a good tone from a battered snare, you can always pound on the local telephone book.   •

FIG. 1 (left)
Two condenser mics placed in a crossed pattern behind the drummer's ears provide an alternative to traditional overhead mic placements. This "drummer's perspective" offers the advantage of producing sharp cymbal timbres *and* robust tom sounds with just two mics.

FIG. 2
A single, large-diaphragm condenser mic placed at chest level about ten feet in front of the drum kit produces a sonic snapshot of the drum/room environment.

Ultimate Bass Tracks

HERE'S THE SCOOP on rhythm tracks: A crummy guitar timbre can be distorted, flanged into respectability, or hidden far beneath the sonic textures of a mix. Likewise for lame keyboard pads. But attempting to foist a wrecked bass tone upon a recording is like trying to hide a buffalo inside a baggie: It can't be done.

The bass is part of the holy rhythm section. Obviously, the bass and drums must lock together in a passionate *danse du beat*, or you've got no track. But many recordists forget that the sound of the rhythm section can be just as important as its performance. A wimpy bass tone sabotages the impact of a relentless beat. In short, if it doesn't pump, it's junk.

"BASS-IC" IMPACT

Ugly bass tones spring from compromised signals. Classic instruments, such as the Fender Precision and the Hofner "Beatle bass," often have poorly shielded electronics that add annoying hums, hiccups, or RF waves to the signal. However, if the audible level of the malady is tastefully discreet, the unwanted noise may be hidden in the sonic wash of the overall mix. There's no sense obsessing over a minute detail that's fated for obliteration under 40 tracks of distorted guitars.

For instance, audible hiss seldom is an issue, because the critical frequencies for meaty bass tones lie far below the hiss strata. Simply use your console EQ to cut frequencies above 10 kHz, and the hiss factor should disappear without compromising the fundamental bass sound.

RF waves are a more virulent problem, because they can be as audible as the bass signal itself. Noise gates or manual signal muting can't eradicate RF engine whines if the anomaly appears when the instrument is playing. (Obviously, muting the RF signal also kills the bass signal.) Positioning often is the only cure. The idea is to find a spot where the instrument is less effective as an RF antenna. Have the bassist turn in different directions until the whining stops. Tape the floor to identify the "safe zone," and threaten physical violence if the bassist moves off the mark during his or her performance. If RF waves invade every position, find a better shielded bass.

THE DIRECT ROUTE

The easiest way to record an electric bass is through a direct connection to the recording console. If you're running a -10 dBV unbalanced system, you can plug the 1/4-inch cable from the bass right into a mixer line input. However, a more robust signal can be gained by utilizing a direct box—an essential tool for interfacing with +4 dBu balanced systems—to run through a microphone input. (Mic inputs typically provide more gain than line inputs.)

by Michael Molenda

For demo projects, the "naked" direct method provides a good enough sound to document sonic and musical arrangements. However, the tight, visceral punch of professional bass tracks is difficult to achieve without compression. There are a number of great compressors on the market. Some of my favorites (applicable to home or project studio use) include the dbx 166, the Symetrix 425, and UREI's tube 1176. In addition, many bass amplifiers have built-in compressors and line outputs to facilitate direct recording.

Because direct recording tends to highlight performance blemishes—there's no amp/speaker/room environment to cloak fret noise and sloppy dynamics—it's important to match compression parameters to the sonic demands of both the track and the bassist's technique. Audio empathy requires critical listening and intuitive processing, but I often invoke basic settings as starting points.

If a player has excellent tone and technique, I may tame only the odd dynamic peak with a -10 dB compression threshold at a 2:1 ratio. Mid-level bassists usually require more help to achieve a smooth, round tone, so the settings are upgraded to a -15 dB threshold at a 4:1 ratio. Seamlessly tight bass lines (or technically deficient players) can be recorded by crushing the signal under a -20 dB threshold at a 12:1 ratio. However, be careful with the high numbers: Heavy compression often emphasizes low frequencies. If over-compression turns your signal into mud, you can retrieve some snap with your console EQ by cutting at least 3 dB from 100 Hz.

Many dedicated bass preamps allow controlled direct recording. These units are not as plentiful as guitar-oriented devices, but who says you can't run a bass through a guitar preamp? During a session with San Francisco's preeminent progressive rock band Zircus, noted producer Scott Mathews recorded a tortured, funky bass line through a SansAmp.

GETTING AMPED

One thing direct recording can't deliver is the sound of an 18-inch speaker pumping bass into a room. Unfortunately, documenting an amplified performance requires a good amp and speaker combi-

ALAN SILFEN

nation, good microphones, and tolerant neighbors.

A typical project studio setup (**Fig. 1**) utilizes an enclosed room or isolation booth as a "bass trap" to prevent low frequencies from dissipating in an open acoustic environment. I usually position a large-diaphragm dynamic microphone—my favorites are the Electro-Voice RE20 and the Sennheiser MD 421—approximately six inches from the center of the bass speaker cone. If the speaker enclosure has mid-frequency horns, I don't mike them. Moving the mic farther back from the bass speaker usually provides a sufficient mix of low-frequency booms and midrange articulation.

To record the bass-enhanced room tone, I position an AKG C414 condenser mic ten feet away from the amp, at a height of about seven feet. (Whatever

The cute Beatle with his classic Hofner "Beatle" bass (a set list from an early-1960s Fab Four concert remains taped to the side of the instrument). Paul McCartney's booming melodic tone still inspires bassists of all stylistic disciplines. The closest I've gotten to reproducing McCartney's wonderfully warm bass tone is mixing a direct signal with a miked bass amp. I use the direct signal for articulation and boost the lows on the amp sound to provide warmth.

FIG. 1
Mammoth bass tones can be recorded by enclosing an amplifier in a sealed room. Employing close-miked and room-mic positions gives recordists the option of processing two diverse source sounds.

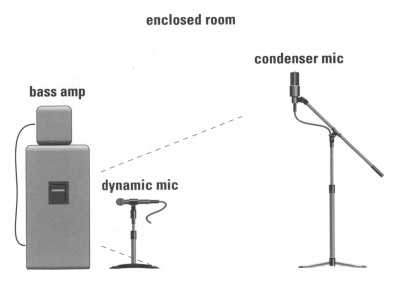

enclosed room

condenser mic

bass amp

dynamic mic

model of condenser you use, be sure to protect its diaphragm by padding the mic at least -10 dB.) The close-miked and room sounds can be routed to separate mixer input channels and submixed to a mono bass track, or recorded onto two individual tracks for stereo imaging.

Home recordists can transform an enclosed closet into a neighbor-friendly bass trap. First, purchase enough three-inch-thick foam (check out bedding and military supply shops) to cover the closet's rear and side walls to a height of approximately four feet. The foam needn't be permanently attached; you can lean it against the walls or tape it in place. Leave your clothes on their hangers to provide additional sound absorption, but remove belts or other accessories that may rattle during tracking.

Now place a small "practice" bass amp or guitar amp—a compact model with a single 12- or 15-inch speaker is perfect—inside the foam womb, with the speaker facing the closet door. Position a mic directly in front of the speaker and close the door.

Because you're downsizing a commercial recording environment, you shouldn't need a lot of amp volume to emulate a suitable "boom room." A few tweaks of the amp's tone controls often is all that's required to evoke a punchy bass track.

COMBINATION PLATE

Sometimes a direct or amp sound alone doesn't cut it. Direct bass signals can sound a tad sterile, and amp tones often venture into the muddy side of the sonic spectrum. What's an engineer to do? Luckily, a simple direct box is the key to accentuating the positive attributes of the two source signals (**Fig. 2**).

Plug the bass into the ¼-inch instrument jack of the direct box (the normal connection for direct recording) and connect a balanced XLR cable from the direct box to your mixer. Then run a ¼-inch cord from the amp jack of the direct box into your amplifier's input jack. Now, position a microphone in front of the amp's speaker cabinet and route the mic cable to another input on your mixer. *Voilà!* You have two sound sources on two separate mixer inputs. You can submix the two sounds to a mono track, or

record both bass tracks and postpone sonic decisions until the final mix. The two tracks also can provide a stereo effect.

Combining an amp and direct sound can revitalize lackluster bass tracks. This approach literally saved the rhythm tracks during my production of a label-development demo for San Francisco's Bolshoi Rodeo, an alternative country act. The group's bassist had great musical ideas, but her tentative technique produced an indistinct and dynamically erratic signal.

TIMOTHY WHITE

I was loathe to hire a session player, because Bolshoi's bassist was also the lead vocalist and obviously had a special understanding for the band's material. As a "last chance," I tried using a direct signal and an amp miked via the bass-trap configuration, with close and room mics. For maximum effect, I treated each of the three signals differently: The direct signal

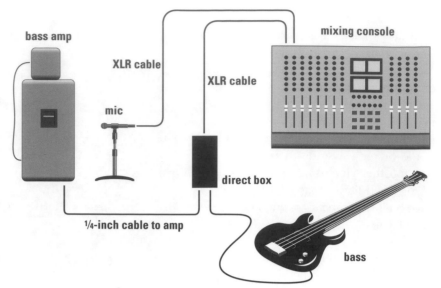

FIG. 2
Combining a clean, direct sound with the sonic impact of an amplifier's roar often energizes a bass track.

Tina Weymouth has traversed a lot of stylistic territory in her career with Talking Heads and Tom Tom Club. Likewise, a well-rounded engineer should be aware of the sonic demands of different types of music. A hardcore punk band might want the bass sound to be a low-end rumble, while a funk bassist might ask for heavily articulated mids.

was flat (no EQ), the close mic was cut at the low-mids and boosted at 100 Hz, and the room mic was drastically cut at 10 kHz, left flat along the low-mids, and boosted at 100 Hz.

The three signals were submixed to mono, with a compressor in-line at the subgroup insert point. Fader levels for the direct and room mic signals were almost equal (favoring the room sound), with the speaker mic mixed in to add subtle midrange frequencies. The compressor was set to ruthlessly tame dynamic levels, posting a -25 dB threshold with a slow release at a ratio of 10:1.

What resulted from all this trouble was a huge, booming Phil Spector rumble devoid of (noticeable) fret squeaks, yet punchy enough to articulate harmonic movement. The thick bass sound complemented the sharp attack of the drums and provided a perfect foil for the band's acoustic guitars and delicate vocals. I had stumbled upon one of those rare marvels of sonic design: a sound so rooted in the individual personality of a recording that it transcends its primary function of masking a player's technical foibles.

HOME BASS

As revealed in *Rock on the Road*, a British book about the music industry that was published in the 1970s, the "genius" of glam-rock band Slade was that their records were produced to feature the bass lines when the tracks were played at loud volumes. Supposedly, the enhanced bass made Slade records a hot commodity in discos.

Let's forget the fact that even a James Taylor record played at extreme dance-club volumes will produce deep bass tones. (The human ear's sensitivity to bass frequencies increases with volume.) The point is, the *perception* of a driving bass tone is crucial to the rhythmic ideals of rock, rap, dance, salsa, and other popular music styles. Slade's historian knew this, even if he did mistake physics for audio wizardry.

What does this anecdote teach us about bass tracks? Well, besides the fact that a music critic should *never* understand more about the magic of making records than you, it shows that cool records always have great-sounding bass lines. The pop graveyard is chock-full of lifeless rhythm sections. So don't spare the intensity as you struggle to produce a killer bass tone. The public can deliver hard and fickle judgments, and there are always people standing in line to bite the hand that bores them.   •

John Patitucci is one of the young techno-giants of modern jazz. His fluidity on the six-string bass is awesome, and he's charted a number one album on the *Billboard* jazz charts and earned a Grammy nomination. When I work with technical monsters, I usually record them flat (no EQ) and trust them to deliver the tonal goods. Sometimes the best way to record great sounds is to step back and let the player rip.

Ultimate Guitar Tracks

A FEW YEARS AGO, a national music magazine published an article on "recording tips." The author gave specific instructions, right down to the equalization settings, for achieving great guitar, bass, and drum sounds. Call me irresponsible, but I tore the magazine into confetti and torched the sucker. I detest simple, step-by-step tutorials that reduce the pursuit of a creative discipline to a no-brainer. (Hey, professional audio engineering now is easier than programming your VCR!)

Recording great sounds is not as easy as 1-2-3. Getting magnificent guitar noises on tape requires good ears, ingenuity, and the ability to concentrate on minute nuances of sound. Technical manuals sometimes forget that audio engineering is an art form of calculated anarchy, with few rules and no limits. This freedom drives recording engineers to produce sounds that are clearer, more evocative, and just plain weirder than the existing sonic palette. But you can kiss *your* future timbral discoveries goodbye if you let a book tell you how to tweak a guitar sound.

So here's the deal: This chapter won't chart the EQ slope of Eric Clapton's lead tone, expose The Edge's delay parameters, or measure the distance from the amp of a "proper" room mic. I'll toss out some concepts behind professional guitar tracking and let you run with them.

The prime directive is to trust your ears. Happy hunting!

THE SANCTITY OF THE SOURCE

Microphones are not magic wands. Inspired miking of a poor guitar or guitar/amp combination only serves to record a bad sound exceptionally well. Too many musicians and engineers, seduced by the methodology of recording—mic selection, mic placement, gain stages, equalization, and signal processing—forget to scrutinize what is being recorded. Like Humpty Dumpty, all the technological wonders in the audio kingdom can't save a vile source sound.

For example, if you record an acoustic guitar in a bathroom (often the premier "isolation booth" of the home studio), sympathetic sound reflections might cause the instrument to appear unnaturally metallic or boomy. But don't expect EQ adjustments or mic placement to solve your tonal problems. No matter how many knobs you turn (or mics you move), your source sound will remain compromised by its poor acoustic environment. The best thing to do is to make the bathroom more hospitable for recording. A "quick fix" might involve draping a few blankets around to absorb the impish reflections. If the sound still is less than beautiful, you can hire an acoustical

by Michael Molenda

contractor to remodel your bathroom or simply seek a more complementary recording environment.

Room acoustics are not the only sonic booby-traps awaiting the recordist. Be sure to check for anomalies haunting the guitar itself: fret buzzes, dead strings, poor intonation, and so on. The easiest way to "fix" a crummy guitar is to beg, borrow, or steal a good one. However, if you're stuck with a sonic dysfunction, remedies are available.

Lifeless strings can be punched up by compressing the guitar during recording. Simply put, a compressor can raise the levels of weak signals to produce a smoother, more robust sound. Start with a basic setting of a -10 dB input threshold at a 2:1 ratio, and continue to tweak the compression parameters until the strings sound tight and even. You also may have to adjust the EQ on the board to compensate for increased bass response. (The relative level of low frequencies often increases when a signal is compressed.) It doesn't hurt to add a little sparkle by boosting the midrange frequencies; just take care not to increase audible hiss by overdoing it.

Acoustic guitars with annoying fret buzzes often can be tamed with a de-esser. This device, usually employed to diminish sibilant vocals, sometimes can stifle fret sizzles enough to allow passable tracking. Intonation problems are tough calls. You can attempt subtle mixtures of pitch-shifting (chorus, flange, phase, etc.) along with the fundamental

sound, but the result seldom appears natural when foisted on acoustic instruments. If the guitar won't stay in tune, the best remedy is to find a more disciplined instrument. Adding modulation to smear dysfunctional tonalities works better with electric guitars, because massive signal processing often is a major component of the "plugged in" sound.

Speaking of electric guitars, adding an amplifier to the source sound equation can be a nightmare. Amp and guitar combos sometimes produce a symphony of hisses, hums, rattles, and buzzes. Luckily, this sonic hullabaloo usually is masked by the sound of the guitar. However, I don't like to hear junk before song introductions and during passages where the guitarist is not playing. A noise gate is a wonderful tool to help clean up these sections. Simply set the gate's input threshold to shut down the guitar signal when there is no performance. (Be careful that the gate isn't so eager that it cuts out a player's softer dynamics.) If hiss is so virulent that it *is* audible during performance, try using a single-ended noise reduction device—such as the dbx 563 Silencer or Rocktron's Hush—in addition to the noise gate.

PLACE SETTINGS

Zealots often discuss mic placement as if it were the holy grail of sound recording. They're absolutely right. The relatively simple procedure of positioning a microphone where it "hears" the best sound

Bonnie Raitt proved that blues licks and slide guitar don't have to dump an artist in the cult status trap. Her bluesy chops and roadhouse persona didn't stop her from scoring a well-deserved string of massive hits in the early 1990s.

DEBORAH FRANKEL

Marc Bolan's (far left) funky and fragmented rhythm chops made him one of the most identifiable and influential guitarists of 1970s. The Metal Guru's searing guitar tone was produced by his omnipresent Gibson Les Paul plugged into a tube amp—typically a Marshall or Orange stack—turned "full up."

In the 1990s, Lenny Kravitz (shown here doing a pretty mean Marc Bolan imitation) proved that "what goes around, comes around" by charting hits shrouded in sonic nostalgia.

separates great engineers from audio dilettantes.

Good mic placement requires cognitive hearing. The trick is to visualize yourself as a microphone, using your ears to approximate what the transducer will record on tape. The closer you get to your idealized sound through mic placement, the less you'll rely on equalization and signal processing. The result is a cleaner signal with maximum impact.

MIKING ACOUSTIC GUITARS

The dominant tonality of an acoustic guitar usually is found approximately six inches over the sound hole. Brighter, more articulated timbres often appear closer to the bridge and along the fretboard. A single condenser microphone, such as an AKG C414, often does a great job of reproducing the shimmering timbres of a fine guitar. Use your ears to determine the best mic position, but avoid placing the mic directly over the sound hole, because the resonance can muddy bass tones.

A stereo effect can be recorded by positioning two mics to reproduce different tonalities from a single guitar. The classic position is where one mic is pointed toward the bridge (for sparkling articulation) and another toward the sound hole (for warmth and "body"). I employ condenser mics for this application, but I don't use a matched set of identical models. I've found the tonal variance (and therefore the stereo effect) is intensified when different mics are used. I often mismatch an AKG C414 with an Audio-Technica AT4033 or a Sony ECM33F.

If you desire a more spacious sound, set up a condenser mic on a boom stand and position it far forward and above the guitarist. This room perspective can be recorded onto a separate track for a hard stereo effect (close mic sound left/dreamy room sound right), or mixed into the primary acoustic guitar sound.

I enjoy the sound of naked acoustic guitars, so I don't often dress them up with signal processing. However, I can't resist stacking unison tracks to construct an orchestra of strumming guitars. (Thank

you, Phil Spector.) Obviously, the more tape (or digital) tracks you have at your disposal, the more intense this effect becomes. I typically submix six to eight tracks down to stereo, although in a tremendous lapse of reason I once submixed 15 tracks to mono. Compression is always employed to tame wayward dynamics for a harmonious blend.

MIKING ELECTRIC GUITARS

A single dynamic mic pointed dead center at a guitar speaker is the classic rock and blues position (**Fig. 1**). Practically the entire history of rock guitar sounds is written in the space between a Shure SM57 microphone and a Marshall or Fender amplifier. This position offers an accurate representation of the sound of the guitar and amp, because the close proximity of the mic to the speaker eliminates much of the personality of the room.

The re-emergence of funk players in the mid-1980s popularized an interesting turn on the single mic technique. The off-axis position (**Fig. 2**) accentuates the jewel-like tones of a clean, undistorted guitar while still producing a sharp, aggressive sound. Condenser microphones work best for off-axis applications because they emphasize the crystalline timbres.

Of course, the sky is the limit for some engineers. I've witnessed sessions where both speakers of a 2 x 12-inch, open-back cabinet were close-miked front and back, stereo room mics were positioned behind and in front of the amp, and stereo mics were mounted on the ceiling.

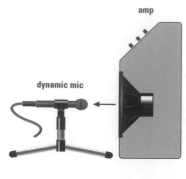

FIG. 1
The classic team of a dynamic microphone and a tube amp is hard to beat when seeking the ultimate electric guitar sound.

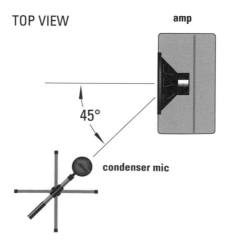

FIG. 2
Off-axis mic positions favor the tough, crystalline tones popularized during the late-1980s funk revival.

The classic room mic setup (**Fig. 3**) is a much simpler way to mix an acoustic environment with the source sound.

AXING THE AMP

The bell is tolling for the guitar amp. Speaker simulators, amp emulators, and rackmount preamps are sending our trusty Marshalls and Fenders down the path of the typewriter. I can already see the day when old-timers and retro wackos lug around combo amps with the nostalgic fervor of a World War II veteran stuffed into 50-year-old olive drabs.

I don't believe these emulating up-starts sound as wonderful as the real thing yet, but it's difficult to deny their practicality. Electric guitars are noisy by nature, and if your home studio is an apartment, a live amp is a quick ticket to eviction. A good amp or speaker simulator makes it possible to record "loud" guitar sounds direct: no microphones, no 120 dB concussion zones, and you can monitor at neighbor-friendly volumes (or through headphones). In addition, setup and sound-tailoring time is slashed, because these units are designed to plug in and play.

My personal favorites are speaker emulators such as Marshall's SE100 and PS System's Power Tool, because they let me use my own amp. All my familiar settings are available, but I don't have to hassle with microphones, because these devices route the amp signal directly to the mixer. Once the speaker output of an amp head is plugged into such a unit, the signal is brought down to line level and imped-ance is tracked like a real loudspeaker. The result is a "direct" sound that emu-lates the timbre of your amp close-miked through a quality microphone. There's no room environment, of course, because you've eliminated the room sound along with the mic. A little reverb is all that's needed to replace the missing ambience. However, I often like the dry tone so much that I let it rage unprocessed.

On the amp emulation front, Tech 21's versatile SansAmp is a favorite of home recordists and project studio owners. The device comes in rackmount and floor-pedal models, and emulates the sound of

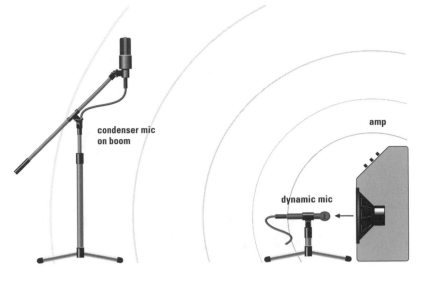

classic amplifiers with the flick of a switch or parameter knob. Also, some multi-effects processors and guitar preamps in-clude amp emulators as standard features. The success rates vary, and few are truly convincing. To be fair, most of these emulators at least *approach* a profes-sional sound, so almost any model is fine for demo use. However, if you plan to cut guitar tracks worthy of a master re-cording, audition these devices with an extremely critical ear.

RIFFING OFF

Guitar sounds are highly personal and tremendously subjective. I love to hear guitarists argue about the definition of a killer guitar sound. Some musicians still worship the pristine perfection of the guitar timbres Roger Nichols engineered for Steely Dan. At the other extreme, Mat-thew Sweet's *Girlfriend* al-bum boasts the crudest demo-level guitar sounds I've ever heard. The won-derful thing is that each sound fits flawlessly into the sonic landscapes of these disparate artists. Dis-covering sounds that en-hance an artist's musical vision should be Job One for creative engineers and pro-ducers. And there's no way I can tell you that this musical sensitivity is attained by cut-ting 6 dB at 15 kHz. •

FIG. 3
Expansive guitar sounds are captured by positioning a condenser mic to record the room environment, while a conventional close-miked per-spective handles the amp tim-bres.

The multi-talented T-Bone Burnett is one of the folk-influ-enced rockers who made acoustic guitars "cool" again in the late 1980s. His spar-kling but tough timbres proved that acoustic guitars could be just as heavy as their electric counterparts.

FRANK GARGANI

Ultimate Synth Tracks

TEMPTATION CAN BE DANGEROUS. The glistening technology of digital synthesizers often seduces recording engineers to route them directly to tape. It's a bad idea. Today's synthesizers make glorious sounds, but a few ugly noises can sneak into the mix if an engineer is not vigilant.

It's important to understand that "CD-quality" digital sound isn't necessarily noise-free. Many factors contribute to a synthesizer's audio hygiene, from the integrity of its PCM samples to its internal circuitry. And remember, while digital sound is touted as immaculate, almost all digital synthesizers convert their information to an analog signal for output. Since many manufacturers seem uninterested in designing clean analog output circuits, their synthesizers sometimes exhibit audible hiss.

HEALTHY SIGNALS

Defensive recording practices can make the difference between a professional-sounding master and a sonically crippled demo tape. The first defense against noise involves getting a clear, robust signal from the synthesizer to the mixer. Healthy levels enhance clarity. A synth's analog signal usually is routed into a mixing console via the line input or through a microphone preamp.

Most digital synthesizers have strong output signals and can be plugged directly into a line input. However, some synthesizers (especially older analog models) have weak signals that require more kick to deliver optimum levels. This can be accomplished by routing the signal through a direct box and plugging into the mixer's microphone preamp. Depending on the mixer, you'll typically gain 20 to 30 dB more level than through the line inputs. Some engineers prefer to use microphone preamps anyway, as they tend to produce a warmer sound.

Be sure to listen critically to all the gain stages between the synthesizer and mixer to protect against unwanted noise. This includes the volume control on the synth itself; some models sound terrible if run "full up." I once spent several minutes tracing the cause of a mangled signal from an expensive digital sound module. Sure enough, when I asked the keyboardist to take his volume down a few notches, the signal changed into a thing of beauty. It pays to experiment with synthesizer and mixer fader levels to ensure a clean signal.

by Neal Brighton

DELICATE EQ

One of the most important things to remember about analog signals is the less you do, the cleaner the signal. Musicians love tweaking equalization, but tonal bliss often is attained with a surcharge of increased hiss. If a string patch isn't "intense" enough, change to a brighter program (or adapt the synthesizer's internal parameters) instead of boosting 10 kHz toward a wash of noise.

If you must change the EQ of the synth sound, you *always* are better off cutting rather than boosting frequencies. For example, if your electric piano patch is too mushy, try cutting some of the bottom end and increasing the overall gain.

DYNAMICS

A problem I encounter constantly when recording synthesizers is their extreme dynamic range. Analog tape hates large differences in signal level. Setting an optimum recording level for one section of a song may risk distortion on another section where the synth really kicks in. If you're firing sound modules from a sequencer, this is remedied by adjusting sensitivity and volume parameters to prevent sudden dynamic changes.

Going to tape is problematic, because the best signal-to-noise ratio is attained by recording the instrument as hot as possible. It is not desirable to set an overall lower recording level to protect against "surprise" peaks, because soft synthesizer passages will be recorded low enough to invite unwanted tape hiss. However, it's madness to track level changes by constantly adjusting the mixer's input faders. The easiest solution is to run the synthesizer through a compressor. A compressor limits the instrument's dynamic range and allows you to get a stronger level to tape without distortion. Try starting out with a input threshold of -10 dB, with a fast attack and a 2:1 signal ratio. From there, tweak the compression parameters until *all* performance levels are "smoothed out" enough to permit setting a safe and reasonable recording level. Don't forget to check that the compressor hasn't added any dirt to your (hopefully) pristine synth signal. Also, compression tends to bring up a signal's bass frequencies, so you may want to audition the processed tone to ensure that it's what you want.

NOISE GATES

Sometimes audible hiss enters the signal path regardless of how much care is exercised. In these instances, noise gates

become essential studio tools. Basically, these units shut down any signals below a user-set threshold. Since audible hiss usually is at a softer level than the actual synthesizer sound, the noise gate can eliminate hiss whenever the instrument stops playing. (Hopefully, the hiss is masked when the synthesizer is playing. If not, try cutting some of the high frequency EQ.)

I can't stress how important it is to keep tracks clean when a particular instrument is silent. If you're running ten ungated synthesizers that pop in and out of a composition at different times, the audible hiss produced by "silent" modules can be high enough to compromise overall quality.

In addition, a gated synth appears in the soundscape with more apparent dynamic punch than an ungated synth that must rise from the muck of constant audible hiss. If you submix multiple synthesizer sounds (playing the same part) for textural emphasis, remember to insert the noise gate at the appropriate subgroup of your mixing console so that all sounds are gated at the same time.

If audible hiss still is apparent during the performance of a sound (some patches are just plain noisy), single-ended noise reduction can save the day. There are many different models on the market. (The dbx 563x and Rocktron's Hush are common commodities in home and project studios.) Basically, what these units do is reduce background hiss by diminishing treble frequencies that exist *above* the fundamental sound source. Keep in mind that these units will affect the overall high-end sound of the synthesizer. Since this may wipe out the desirable shimmer of a patch along with the hiss, single-ended noise reduction should be used sparingly.

TRACK STACKS

There is more to a great synthesizer sound than cleanliness. If you really want to construct masterful timbres, you have to stack two or more different sound modules. While stacking synth sounds via a MIDI sequencer is great for creating

ADRIAN BOOT

Remember when synthesizers had programming knobs? Steve Winwood, whose commercial "comeback" in the 1980s was fueled by sensual layers of synthesized soul, is shown toiling in the days before nested parameter menus.

JAY BLAKESBERG

The early progressive rock movement, with its reliance on classical and jazz idioms, enlarged the popular scope of the synthesizer. One of the most accomplished—and distinguished—of those pioneers is Tony Banks of Genesis.

pads and solo sounds, many keyboard players and producers have gone back to old-fashioned "performance" stacking. This is where a keyboard player actually plays a part (or parts) two or more times onto separate tracks. The engineer then submixes these tracks either to a mono track or to two tracks for a stereo (left/right) split.

The reason this organic method is gaining popularity is the difference in sound between programmed (and quantized) MIDI stacking and stacked performance tracks. The performed tracks have minor differences in timing—after all, humans *aren't* machines—and these anomalies often fatten up the overall sound. Sure, you can play the same parts into a sequencer without quantization, but there usually remains a subtle stiffness. Use your discretion as to which method best enhances a particular composition.

Another stacking trick is to use different sounds for each pass. Since most keyboard manufacturers provide two or three varieties of the same sound ("strings," for instance), it makes sense to mix and match timbres to create thicker and more vibrant textures.

If you mix sequenced virtual tracks with analog tape tracks, try using different synthesizers for stereo images, rather than internal stereo patches. Many synthesizers use a fixed delay to create the right- or left-hand sound of their stereo output. This often is not a sweeping dimensional evocation. Since it is easy to find similar sounds from many different keyboard manufacturers, a more intense stereo image can be gained simply by placing one manufacturer's synthesizer on the left side and a different synthesizer model on the right side.

"EFFECTATIONS"

A common engineering and production concern is whether it's practical to print effects to tape along with the synth sound. From a purely engineering standpoint, this is a risk, since the processed sound cannot be changed once it is recorded. (Considering how often a musician changes his or her mind, it's a *big* risk.) In my opinion, if your outboard gear is sparse and you really can commit

to a particular sound, it makes sense to save mixing aggravation by printing a processed sound to tape. After all, the worst-case scenario is that you'd have to replay the part in question.

Signal processing also can bestow stereo imaging upon old analog synthesizers with mono outputs. (This method also works if track assignments limit you to a mono keyboard track.) Simply route the synth's mono signal into a delay processor and set the delay time to approximately 30 milliseconds. This timing should "clone" the original synth sound. Then, pan the original signal to the left and return the delayed signal to an available input channel or effects return. Pan the delayed signal to the right, and there you have it: a faux stereo image from a mono signal. Also, playing with longer delay times can create interesting "ping-pong" images that headphone listeners will love.

If you are uncomfortable diving into synth sound programming, signal processing allows another path to unique sound construction. Many sound mutations can be enacted by simply running the synth signal through a chorus or pitch shifter. Don't fall victim to Preset Syndrome. Why cheapen your artistry with the same sound that appears on diaper commercials? If you can't program, process.

FINAL OUTPUT

Creating great synthesizer sounds on tape is not hard; it just takes imagination and a commitment to cleanliness. I'm always shocked at the number of demo tapes I hear that are compromised by noisy tracks. As soon as I hear a storm of hiss rise up from a demo cassette, I can't help but rate it an amateur effort. Label executives—whose car CD players provide them with a constant and critical sonic reference—probably draw the same conclusion. And anyway, why would anyone want hiss and audio muck to co-exist with a brilliantly conceived and performed musical work? To me, that would be like da Vinci tossing mud on the Mona Lisa. •

Starr Parodi plays in one of the coolest groups ever to blast out over late-night television: the Arsenio Hall band. Parodi also is a sequencing whiz who uses a laptop Atari STacy4 computer as part of her stage rig.

Although Herbie Hancock (shown above stepping center stage with a portable "strap-on" keyboard) is a respected progressive jazz artist, he has made a few successful forays into the pop/crossover market. Hancock arguably kicked the 1980s synth-rock scene into high gear when his instrumental dance track "Rockit" became a mega-hit in 1983.

A Multitude of Voices

A TRUE STORY: Many years ago, Paul McCartney produced an album for his younger brother, who avoided apple-to-apple comparisons by calling himself Mike McGear. During a vocal session, Paul ordered a large cardboard box brought to the studio. Imagine the nervous glances when Paul grabbed a microphone, climbed inside the box with wife (and background vocalist) Linda, and started to sing! I can just hear Mac #1 assuring his brother, "Don't worry, mate, this is how we cut all those Beatles records." (Well, maybe Ringo's tunes.)

The moral of this story is that whatever works, works. Paul's cardboard isolation booth probably horrified the session engineer, but may have produced a strange and wonderful vocal sound. (Unfortunately, history is hazy on this one.)

Admittedly, the law of averages is on the side of conventional recording practices. Industry standards have been honed by decades of trial and error, and the unassailable fact is that professional methods yield professional results. But the path of convention is not the only road to great sound, and the mix of imagination and technique is never more critical than when recording vocals.

ALIVE AND KICKING

Sometimes the best method of recording a great vocal performance is to stay out of the way. Even Mitch Miller was hip to this. Miller was a squatty cat with a Van Dyke beard who produced some incredibly foul *Sing Along with Mitch* records in the 1960s. When Miller heard a sound he liked, he instructed the recording engineer to freeze. Once, an engineer objected to the command, complaining that the VU meters were pinned at distortion levels. Miller simply ordered the uptight knob-twister to cover the meters with masking tape so that no one could see them. The moral here is that Miller trusted his ears, and so should you. Technological etiquette is fine, but if the sound you hear is glorious, who cares if the tape deck is on fire?

The first step in this organic listening process is to decide whether the vocalist should be recorded live. It is common convention to record lead vocals *after* the rhythm tracks are completed to ensure technical quality, but many vocalists are at their best when singing along with the band. The magic of a guide vocal (cut live to cue the rhythm section) is *by Scott Mathews* often superior to the carefully recorded lead vocal overdub. More "keeper" vocals are cut during the basic tracking sessions than many of us realize.

Some of the great mop-top vocals were recorded live, including "Twist and Shout," "Yesterday," "I Want You (She's So Heavy)," "Let It Be," and "The Long and Winding Road." The King (Elvis Presley) cut almost everything live. The other Elvis (Costello) often releases tracks containing his impassioned and spontaneous guide vocals, rather than the "proper" overdubbed performances. Even the Chairman of the Board, Frank Sinatra (who does everything his way), insists on cutting his vocals with the band.

A few years ago, I had the pleasure of producing Roy Orbison. He told me that "Pretty Woman" was recorded live in the studio with two drummers pounding and the background vocalist *literally* singing backup: The guy sang over Roy's shoulder into the same microphone. Obviously, the majesty of this track was not compromised by its rough-and-ready recording process.

However, getting good live vocals to tape requires forethought. The optimum situation is to limit unwanted sounds leaking into the vocal microphone by placing the singer in an isolation booth. If this isn't possible, position the drums and amplifiers as far from the singer as possible. Then place baffles around the drums, amps, and vocal microphone. Commercial baffles work the best, but guitar amps can be isolated by draping a heavy blanket over the cabinet. Atco recording artists The Rembrandts used mattresses to isolate unwanted sounds while tracking vocals for their debut album. (In yet another example of what can be accomplished with maximum helpings of

creativity and ingenuity, the Rembrandts' album—which yielded two Top 40 hits—was recorded in a home studio by the two main singer/songwriters.)

Besides its conventional role of deflecting vocal "pops," a windscreen placed in front of the microphone prevents the singer from swallowing or grabbing it during moments of spontaneous abandon. Jim Morrison often was tossed a "fake" mic to manhandle during vocal tracking; the "real" mic was placed above his head. It also helps to roll off a little low end—cutting 5 dB at 100 Hz should do the trick—to diminish the rumble of a band in full swing. If the singer's crooning and screaming fluctuate a little too wildly to permit optimum tracking, route the signal through a compressor to tame the dynamics. A subtle input threshold setting of -10 dB at a 2:1 ratio should do the trick.

THE PROPER TAKE

The conventional option of overdubbing vocal performances onto completed rhythm tracks still requires creative listening. Singers are an intensely individual breed, and a microphone that sounds marvelous on one voice may sound hideous on another. If several microphones are available, be sure to test some to see which sounds best. Once the right microphone is chosen, experiment with miking positions. If you don't have a lot of microphone options, mic placement is critical to achieving good sound. A soul or gospel shouter can send shivers down your spine with the microphone relatively far away, but other stylists may require more proximity.

I often position singers very close to the microphone to achieve an intimate sound. Here's my recipe: Set a condenser microphone on a cardioid or hypercardioid pattern with a -10 dB pad and prop it two inches behind a windscreen. Instruct the singer to put his or her lips right on the windscreen (remember to clean the screen after every session). If the extreme proximity causes pops, lift the microphone up and down a bit until the sound hits the diaphragm from a slight angle. Once the sound is pure, let the singer rip. When the track is com-

PAUL COX

Elizabeth Fraser of the Cocteau Twins often uses her beautifully haunting voice like an electronic instrument. Her lush vocals are typically non-verbal—at least, it's extremely difficult to discern any comprehensible lyrics within her multi-syllabic tone poems—and heavily processed. Sometimes it's fun to "over-process" a vocal with reverb, delay, and/or modulation effects to open up unique sonic frontiers.

HERB RITTS

Okay, no one is going to arrest Madonna for being a transcendent singer. But the "Material Girl" has raised a-t-t-i-t-u-d-e to an art form and has sold millions of albums in the process. To get that perfect attitude on tape, Madonna may sing a song several times onto separate tracks and select the best phrases, words, and even syllables to construct the final composite vocal track.

pleted, audition the performance and punch in lines that need improvement in pitch, phrasing, or intensity.

The improvement process can be overdone. The performances of singers such as Whitney Houston, Madonna, Michael Bolton, and Bono (and I don't mean Sonny) often are polished until they bore me to tears. The voice you hear on the record often is a compilation of endless takes, utilizing the best lines, words, or even syllables to construct a final, perfect vocal take.

GROUP VOX

Recording group background vocals is a relatively easy task. If you desire a room blend of voices, use as many mics as needed and position the singers straight at the mics from a distance of approximately two feet. You also may hang one omnidirectional microphone in the center and have the singers form a "circle of love" around it. But once again, it often pays to seek out the bizarre in order to capture interesting background vocals.

One of the great innovators of strange recording approaches is Brian Wilson. Once, after a leak necessitated draining his swimming pool, Brian placed microphones at the bottom of the deep end and directed the guys to do group vocals lying on their stomachs facing the pool mics. The result can be heard on the album *Smiley Smile*.

Brian's active mind struck again when I recorded with The Beach Boys at Al Jardine's Arabian horse ranch in Big Sur. Since the surroundings were amazing, Brian suggested recording background vocals in the great outdoors. The Beach Boys' recording engineer, Steve Desper, hooked microphones to a horse exerciser, a large, round contraption designed to walk six horses in circles. The apparatus

worked great. Each vocalist had his own mic, eye contact was facilitated by the circular design, and "pet sounds" were provided by horses and birds.

Recording large groups, such as gospel choirs, requires thoughtful administration. The sheer size of these choirs makes it difficult to identify weak performances (or even fit all the singers in the studio). To avoid a nervous breakdown, try recording the vocalists in easily manageable sections: basses, tenors, sopranos, and altos. The different sections can be recorded on separate tracks and then submixed to achieve the desired tonal balance.

JUST MY IMAGINATION...

Recording great vocals is a process limited only by the singer and the imagination of the engineer. The old cliché stands true: "The only rule is, there are no rules." Michelle Shocked recorded her fine premiere album entirely on a Walkman; it may be the only record that actually costs more to buy than it did to make. At the same time, million-dollar releases from industry vets with every hot piece of gear ever invented at their disposal often are virtually unlistenable. Great records are products of the heart; technology is but an accomplice. In the end, the listener cares only about being swept away by a passionate performance. I don't think that the scores of people who bought Beatles records were dying to know which microphones John and Paul used. So don't panic if your imagination leads you into cardboard boxes, entices you to drain the swimming pool, or inspires you to abandon the ordinary.

JEFF KATZ

Jazz vocalist Al Jarreau's trademark scat singing often involves vast dynamic and melodic swoops. A vigilant engineer can avoid tape saturation (or digital distortion) by using a compressor to tame "surprise" signal peaks.

ANDY KENT

David Bowie's vocal style changes almost as often as his stage persona. A typical recording engineer might choose a dynamic mic to track the high-pitched "Ziggy Stardust" Bowie, and rely on a condenser mic to reproduce the dulcet tones of the smooth "Black Tie/White Noise" Bowie.

Recording Unusual Instruments

THERE WAS A KNOCK AT THE STUDIO DOOR and a dozen Balkan-Slavic folk musicians walked in, carrying the strangest instruments I had ever seen. Fighting panic, I could only think of two things: "How do they play these bizarre instruments, and where do I put the microphones?"

No, this wasn't a nightmare. Every recording engineer has a story about having to deal (often unexpectedly) with an unfamiliar or non-traditional instrument. The growing diversity of American pop music continues to introduce folk, ethnic, and classical instruments into the cultural mainstream. For recording engineers, this enlarged musical vocabulary can be intimidating. But in almost every situation, capturing the sound of an unfamiliar instrument is simply a case of getting back to basics.

Don't Panic, Listen!

The guidelines for good engineering don't change just because an instrument is foreign. Listening carefully to the sound source still is the best way to determine an instrument's personality. So before you concern yourself with microphone selection and placement, have the musician play a section of the composition you plan to record. Familiarize yourself with the instrument's tonal range, and identify any sonic peculiarities that might require certain considerations—

perhaps a double windscreen or input padding—to ensure an optimum recording. Don't forget to seek out extraneous noises (creaks, rattles, etc.) that also may compromise the recording.

When you're more familiar with the instrument's "voice," put your ear at the spot where you plan to position the microphone. This simple but often-forgotten procedure should give you some idea what the microphone will hear. Listen for harmonics or other sonic traits that might produce muddy or overly shrill tones. Try to select a microphone that complements the natural sound of the instrument; compensating for a poor mic choice by overdoing it on the EQ can sabotage organic timbres. If you want to maintain authentic tonal colors—especially when recording ethnic instruments—heavy signal processing is a no-no.

Also, don't forget to consider *what* is making the sound. For example, most stringed instruments use resonating soundboards that may or may not have a sound hole. Critical listening is essential, because the "sweet spot" (for mic positioning) can be anywhere along the soundboard.

by Neal Brighton and Michael Molenda

Strange Strings

My Balkan-Slavic friends introduced me to instruments called the prima, the bug, the brac, and the bugaria. Luckily, most stringed instruments—regardless of their cultural origin—are broken up into sections that cover specific octave ranges. Because these sections are similar in concept to Western groupings of violins, violas, cellos, basses, etc., I was able to analyze these bizarre instruments on somewhat familiar ground. I decided to use condenser mics to enhance the bell-like quality of the upper-octave instruments, and dynamic mics to tighten up the low end on the bass instruments.

Certain recording techniques that work for Western stringed instruments also tend to work for other species of the string family. For instance, I made sure the mics weren't placed too close to the musician's hands, to avoid emphasizing percussive sounds during performance. Also, I compressed the signals discreetly to smooth out dynamics. The instruments (and players) tended to produce uneven attacks between strings, which accentuated some notes and muffled others. Compression helped all the notes to ring out with equal clarity, and I don't believe the signal processing compromised the natural tone of the instruments.

One of the most difficult stringed instruments I've recorded is the harp. Besides being large and unwieldy (all harp players seem to drive minivans), harps produce complex overtones, have tremendous melodic and dynamic ranges, and utilize pedals that often thump when depressed. It's a real challenge to get a good harp sound. I've had the best luck with a matched set of condenser mics pointed down from the top of the harp towards the soundboard. The two mics produce a nice stereo image, while the high mic position helps diminish pedal noises.

PREPOSTEROUS PERCUSSION

Ethnic drums, such as the tabla, produce a lot of low frequencies and few overtones. I usually record percussion with a dynamic microphone; the bigger the drum, the larger the diaphragm. Shure SM57s work great on small drums, while an Electro-Voice RE20 or a Sennheiser MD-421 are fine mics for recording big booms. If you want to hear more attack than tone, position the mic approximately one or two inches from the drum skin. If a fuller

sound is more appropriate, pull the microphones back eight to ten inches.

Ambient sounds can be recorded by positioning a condenser microphone a few feet away from the drum. Condenser mics often sound great on drums that produce a lot of overtones. High-frequency percussion instruments (such as

MICHAEL JOYCE

Sam Vudis (bottom row, second from left), director of the Becari Tamburitza Orchestra, and the bizarre collection of bugs, bracs, primas, and other instruments indigenous to Balkan-Slavic folk music.

wind chimes) benefit from small-diaphragm condenser mics such as an AKG C451EB or a capsule from AKG's Blue Line series.

When in doubt, never underestimate the natural sound of the instrument within an ambient environment. Many ethnic drums are meant to be heard in a celebratory milieu, awash in an acoustic whirl of moving bodies and open spaces. A Celtic band once threw down a challenge that I'd never figure out how to record a good sound from their bodhran (a hand drum). They'd been disappointed before, and I determined that other engineers had close-miked the drum. The band was obviously used to hearing the bodhran "live," so I positioned a single AKG C414 approximately four feet in front of the performer. The sound was big and boomy; the band was astonished and happy. (Score one for the Gipper!)

The "live" method also came in handy when recording hand claps, or *palmas*, for a flamenco group. If the mics were placed too close to the performers, the blast of air

Strange instruments often end up in the hands of strange people. This mammoth bass saxophone is held aloft by part-time cowboy and full-time arranger/jazz band leader Frank Macchia (below).

from the fleshy impacts produced audible pops, or the lack of ambience transformed the claps into brittle, dry "snaps." When the microphones were moved back a foot or so from the performers and raised three feet over their hands, the sound was amazing.

WILD WINDS

One of the strangest reed instruments I've recorded is the bass sax. This instrument often is as big as the person blowing into it. It also produces a tremendous amount of air. I selected an AKG C414 condenser mic to enhance the saxophone's meaty low tones. The majority of a reed instrument's sound is from the bell—which can focus one hell of a rush of air at the mic—so I padded the microphone -10 dB *and* used a windscreen to protect the C414 from the instrument's elephant-like bellow.

The Japanese shakuhachi flute is another difficult wind instrument to record, due to the amount of air rushing through its long wooden cylinder. I've never found it pleasing to put a microphone too

CHRISTOPHER WATT

close. I usually find the best sound is captured by placing a condenser microphone a few feet away from the performer. This ambient position minimizes fingering and breath noises and adds a pleasing room tone. This method also works well with traditional flutes and recorders.

I'd thought I'd heard everything until a local ballet company wanted to record a performance soundtrack with a didjeridu player. This long, often beautifully carved wooden tube developed by Australian aborigines is the Tasmanian devil of musical instruments. The didjeridu explodes with sonic vortexes of grunts, howls, rumbles, whistles, and just about everything else you'd hear in the Australian wilderness.

It was obvious that this wild beast would obliterate any microphone crazy enough to get close. Fine. I positioned the player in a tile hallway and placed an AKG C414 far above her on a stairwell. Then, to accentuate the didjeridu's chaotic rumbles, I placed a pressure zone microphone on the tile floor, approximately three feet from the end of the instrument. The combination of the microphones, the live recording environment, and the omnidirectional caterwaul of the didjeridu combined to produce a magnificent effect. Actually, most of the final sound was derived from the "stair" mic, because the pressure zone mic tended to reproduce shrill tones.

BACK TO NORMAL

Unusual instruments don't have to jerk a recording session into high-stress mode. Just about every instrument, no matter how alien, has a timbral similarity to a more familiar sound. The trick is to calm down and trust your ears. Also, the performer often can help put things in perspective by relating how he or she has recorded the instrument in the past. If the player insists on a specific microphone and/or mic position, it might behoove you to go with the flow (unless you can instantly produce a better sound). If you don't lose your head, you should be able to record an entire armada of Balkan-Slavic folk musicians without breaking a sweat. •

Ambience often is important when recording ethnic instruments. The pastoral melodies of shakuhachi flutist John Singer would sound unnatural close-miked in a "dead" isolation booth.

The classical harp may evoke images of heaven's angels, but getting it to sound great on tape can require a season in hell. Careless microphone placement can inflict pedal thumps and creaks upon shimmering performances from modern harpists such as Boris Goldmund (far left).

Sampling Reality

IT'S DIFFICULT TO IMAGINE A WORLD WITHOUT SAMPLING. Nearly every synthesizer sold today is based around a set of samples, and stand-alone samplers continue to be highly prized instruments. But in spite of this, most musicians are not well-versed in the sampling process. They typically cite the common perceptions that it's difficult, time-consuming, and a hassle to create your own samples. What they tend to forget (or simply don't know) is how rewarding the experience can be.

Of course, producing great samples *isn't* easy. There are no shortcuts to perfection. And the effort you'll expend creating your own samples may get harder and harder to justify, since today's instruments offer vast menus of good-quality sampled sounds. But you'll never produce the sounds you hear in your head unless you dig in and realize them yourself. If you're a sonic adventurer, sampling can be a wonderfully intoxicating discipline. The payoff is that the more you work at it, the higher your standards will become, and the better your samples will sound.

CAPTURING THE INSTRUMENTS

Unless your closest friends happen to play strings, brass, or woodwinds, my advice is to hire the best musician you can possibly afford for your sampling session and record their efforts on tape.

It's not necessary to find someone who is guest soloing with the London Symphony, but they *do* need to be able to produce a clear, consistent tone across the full range of the instrument.

Before starting to record, spend some time explaining to the performers exactly what is expected. Tell them you need a two- to three-second recording of each chromatic note the instrument can produce, with consistent attack and articulation. Keep in mind that what is consistent enough for the player may not be consistent enough for sampling purposes. I recommend getting two or three takes of each note; there always will be one that is better than the others and matches the samples above and below it more closely.

At this point, you need to decide if you want the instrumentalist(s) to play with or without natural vibrato. The bottom line is that for some instruments (bowed strings and flutes, for example), there is just no way an LFO can reproduce the richness of real vibrato. On the other hand, samples of reed instruments—oboes, English horns, saxophones, etc.—and many brass instruments, including trumpets and trombones, can deliver a pretty convincing vibrato if you add just a little filter and amplitude modulation, along with pitch modulation. Sections always should be recorded with at least a small amount of vibrato. This technique

by Jim Miller

usually makes it easier to loop your final sample, because you can loop on a natural, cyclical event.

MICS AND PLACEMENT

While I always advise using the best mic you can lay your hands on, you don't need to own the world's most expensive mics to create great samples. Even when I've had the opportunity to use top-of-the-line B&Ks and Neumanns, I always come back to my AKG C414s (which aren't exactly dogmeat, of course). I know what I can expect of them, I've worked with them for years, and I know where to place them to get the best sound.

Mic placement is a complex subject, but here are a few suggestions for particular instruments. If you're sampling a trumpet or a trombone, place one mic slightly off-axis from the front bell of the horn, about two feet away (**Fig. 1**). Avoid setting the mic directly in front of the horn; this can cause distortion, popping (due to wind exiting from the horn), or a thin and brittle sound. Trumpets and trombones sound best with a little indirect room sound added via a second microphone that is set to an omni or a figure-eight pattern and placed about three feet away.

To sample a flute, place one mic about six inches from the mouthpiece (**Fig. 2**). Avoid setting the mic directly in the path of the player's breath; this can cause horrible rumbling sounds. If possible, use a hypercardioid or cardioid pickup pattern. A second mic can be used on the opposite side of the player, about one foot away (for stereo), or about three to four feet away for more warmth and room sound. Set the second mic to omni or figure-eight.

Cellos record best if you place the first mic about two feet away, slightly below where the player is bowing but pointed into that general area (**Fig. 3**). A second mic should be set on the opposite side, slightly above the instrument but pointed toward the strings. Both mics should be set to a cardioid pattern. As an experiment, try placing the second mic behind the instrument and setting it to an omni pattern.

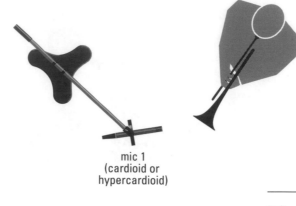

TRUMPET/TROMBONE
overhead view

mic 1
(cardioid or
hypercardioid)

"room sound"
mic 2
(omni)

FIG. 1
To sample a trumpet or trombone, place one mic slightly off-axis from the bell and another a few feet away to pick up room ambience.

For saxophones, one mic should be set about eighteen inches to two feet in front of the instrument, off-axis from the bell (**Fig. 4**). Use a cardioid pickup pattern. For more room sound, put another mic two to four feet away and slightly higher or lower than mic 1. Set it to an omni or figure-eight pattern.

TAPE BACKUP

If you've done much sampling, you know it's important to record onto DAT or some other high-quality, two-track format. Use a good mic preamp and always record in stereo, or with two mics in different positions (i.e., one close to the instrument and another farther away to capture room sound). Even if you're eventually going to create a mono sample, you'll find one mic usually ends up sounding better than the other, and a mix of both mics almost always sounds much better than either mic alone. In addition, sooner or later you will own a sampler with 64-voice polyphony and lots of RAM, and you won't want to re-record the instruments.

In general, I recommend creating mono samples from your stereo source master. Stereo samples require two voices for each note. So if you own a 16-voice Akai S1000, for instance, you will have only eight voices to work with if you use stereo samples. That's far too limiting, especially for instruments that can play more than one note at a time, such as pianos, harpsichords, organs, or guitars. Stereo samples also use twice the memory. I would rather use RAM space to include more samples than devour it with stereo files.

One exception to the mono rule is the drum kit. The acoustic space in which a drum kit is recorded may add a lot of "air," or room feel, to your samples and reduce the need to radically process the final sounds. Eight voices usually are plenty when working with percussion instruments, as they tend to decay rapidly (except for cymbals).

A second exception involves recording sections. With a large string section, for example, the violins are on the left, violas in the middle, and cellos and basses on the right. Depending on your needs, it may make sense to sample them in stereo to preserve that spread, even though this requires sacrificing RAM and polyphony.

One final note: Keep good records of your sessions. I've just started to realize I'm drowning in a sea of poorly labeled or unlabeled DATs. I remember what most of them are, but it would have been much better to label them during the initial sampling session.

DIGITIZING

Now that you've recorded a beautiful set of sounds, all that's left are the most painful, grueling, labor-intensive parts of the process: digitizing and looping.

The way I normally put together a sample set is to start with the lowest note each instrument can sound. From there, I work up the keyboard, sampling as many notes as will fit into RAM. For some difficult instruments (solo violin, for example), I may digitize every note of the first octave or two and then come back and listen critically to determine which samples can be deleted. This process is easy once you have the samples mapped in place, because the "clunkers" stand out quite clearly.

After deleting the samples I don't want, I proceed with the remainder of the notes until I have a complete set of

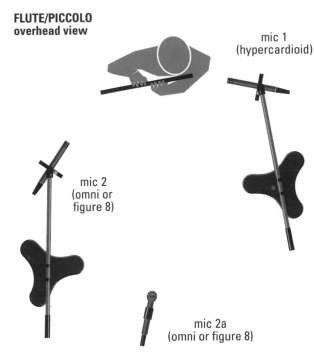

FLUTE/PICCOLO
overhead view

mic 1
(hypercardioid)

mic 2
(omni or
figure 8)

mic 2a
(omni or figure 8)

digitized samples. This process may take a full day or more for some instruments and only a few hours for others. (Saxes and trumpets are particularly easy.) It's always best to have more RAM than you need for the final sample set. By giving yourself a little breathing space, decisions on which samples to delete need not be made too soon. Throughout this entire process, *save to disk often.* Power failures and hardware problems almost invariably occur late in the game, and you'll be a much happier person if you have to digitize only one or two samples instead of fifteen or twenty.

Don't be surprised if after all this effort, you still have one sample that just

FIG. 2 (above)
To capture the breathiness and attack of a flute, place one mic about six inches from the mouthpiece, away from the direct path of the player's breath. Use a second mic up close for stereo, or farther away for more room sound.

FIG. 3 (below)
Cellos are best recorded with one mic about two feet away, slightly in front of the f-holes and bridge, and a second mic just above the instrument. As an alternative, you can try placing the second mic behind the instrument.

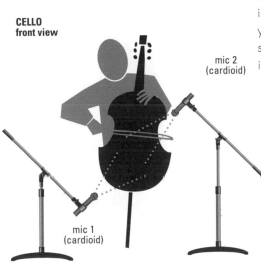

CELLO
front view

mic 2
(cardioid)

mic 1
(cardioid)

doesn't sound quite as good as you'd like, or doesn't match the samples above and below it. Many samplers and computer-based sample editors allow you to pitch-shift a better-sounding sample up or down to replace an unacceptable one. This feature also is useful in extending the range of a sample beyond that of the original instrument (e.g., making a piccolo out of a flute).

One final word about digitizing samples: Though it's nice to have all your samples at a high sample rate, such as 44.1 or 48 kHz, consider using a lower rate to save space. You'd be surprised how few sounds have a lot of high-frequency information above 10 or 12 kHz. I've had surprisingly good results from sampling rates as low as 29 kHz for instruments such as electric guitars, basses, percussion, and certain ethnic instruments.

LOOPING

When I've finished creating the samples for a particular instrument, I stop and save the looping for later. It's much better to begin the looping process with fresh ears.

In truth, the loop points of most instruments will not be readily detectable in multitrack compositions, but you'll feel better if the sample sounds good when played by itself. Most brass and reed instruments, harps, guitars, and tuned percussive instruments such as marimbas and xylophones are easy to loop. Back when we were using 8-bit samplers, single-cycle loops of these instruments were acceptable. Today, short crossfade loops tend to sound the best. In the case of brass and reeds recorded without vibrato, I've found that a quarter-second sample (or even less) is long enough. You want to loop the sound as soon as the initial attack transient has changed over to a fairly consistent waveform, but before there is time for much evolution of the harmonic structure. Harps, marimbas, and xylophones quickly turn into sine waves, which are easy to loop. Acoustic guitars (and some electrics) generally loop well about two or three seconds into the sound and sound pretty good with a fairly short crossfade loop.

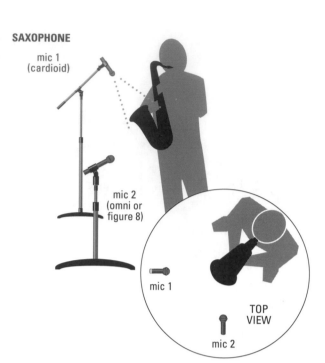

SAXOPHONE

mic 1 (cardioid)

mic 2 (omni or figure 8)

mic 1

TOP VIEW

mic 2

Instruments sampled with vibrato, such as violins or flutes, tend to be a bit tougher to loop, because the amplitude and harmonic structure of each vibrato cycle is likely to be slightly different. Still, with just a touch of crossfading, just about any instrument sampled with vibrato can be looped by placing the start and end points on the peaks or dips of each cycle, about a second and a half into the sample. This should be the point where the player is producing the most consistent vibrato. If your sampler has graphic editing, it is easy to see the best spots to place your loop points.

Much bigger problems present themselves with pianos, pipe organs, distorted guitars, and ensembles. The changing harmonic structures of these sounds do not allow short loops, so you are forced to take a bigger section of the sound and crossfade it. With pianos, a half-second crossfade loop about two or three seconds into the sample works well. The same is true for distorted guitars. Ensembles and pipe organs require grabbing a much bigger chunk of the total sample and doing some liberal crossfading. By the way, of the two crossfade types, *linear* works best with shorter loops in sounds that are decaying, while

FIG. 4
Saxophones record well with one mic about a foot and a half away, slightly off-axis from the bell, and a second mic positioned a few feet off to the side, above or below the first mic.

equal power works best with long loops in sounds that have a lot of harmonic motion.

"REAL WORLD" SAMPLES

Throughout your sampling efforts, it's important to remember that real acoustic instruments (and some electrics) are nothing like synthesizers. Synths can produce a totally uniform sound across the keyboard, but real instruments rarely produce the same tone all the way up and down the full range of the instrument. When sampling real instruments and building your keyboard maps, you need to take this into consideration. There are times when you will have to accept that your samples just won't match up perfectly.

Also, keyboard players are used to hearing a note immediately upon pressing down a key. For some instruments, notably double reeds, breathy saxes, and the lower ranges of most flutes, there is no such thing as an instantaneous attack. For these instruments, the player begins to articulate the note a bit early so that the minute delay will not be noticeable in the performance. To realistically play sampled instruments, you must *think* like the appropriate instrumentalist.

Another "real world" lesson you'll learn is that trial and error often is the truest path towards mastering the art of sampling. After all, even if you fail to produce what you expected, you usually learn many positive things along the way. Producing a great set of samples requires an enormous amount of patience and determination. Those who are quick to criticize anyone's samples only reveal how little they know about the time, effort, and energy that goes into producing them. •

Developing Digital Recording Chops

LESS THAN TWENTY YEARS AGO, Thomas Stockham was a lone voice in the wilderness. The Salt Lake City visionary tried to convince the audio world to accept his Soundstream system, which captured sound using a new and radical method: digital recording.

By and large, the industry regarded Stockham's idea as less than viable. But today, as thousands line up to take home affordable 8-track digital tape or hard-disk recording systems, his vision is unarguably vindicated. Now, however, recordists are faced with mastering the idiosyncrasies of the digital medium.

THE DIGITAL CHALLENGE

Adapting to the digital audio world doesn't have to be a difficult challenge. The nature of digital recording dictates some differences in approach from analog recording, but it also sharpens the focus on many concerns analog recordists have always faced. In particular, the inescapable truth of "garbage in/garbage out" looms large, because the digital medium offers no haven for flaws in the source material or the signal chain.

The scourge of digital recording is noise. Before you even think of pressing the Record button or setting levels, check the noise floor of your recording environment. It's difficult to gauge how much (or how little) your system impacts sonic hygiene unless you complete this simple test: Raise your monitor level to its maximum volume and listen to the amount and quality of noise when there is no signal. Be *extremely* careful. If someone accidentally plays a note while you've got the monitors cranked up, your speakers and ears (as well as your nerves) can be seriously damaged. It's best to test the noise floor before the session begins.

As much as you struggle to record pristine analog tracks, you have to sweat a little harder when recording digitally. No longer can you rely on tape hiss to cover up a noisy microphone or signal processor. To help meet this sonic challenge, manufacturers have developed quieter microphones, microphone preamps, instrument pickups, and even audio cables.

Unfortunately, clean equipment doesn't ensure clean tracks. It's critical that the various gain stages along the signal chain do not add noise. Usually, the first stage—the microphone or line preamp—has the most impact on overall noise performance. But don't stop there. Ascertain which components in your system have the best and worst noise performance and set your levels accordingly. For example, if your mic preamp is noisy when pushed to the max, back it down to a "quieter" setting and use the mixer's mic trim and/or input fader to produce the desired level.

by Larry the O

Of course, critical listening only is helpful if the monitoring environment is good. A computer fan (or other background noise) can mask the fine details you're listening for. Also, having precise monitor speakers is imperative. What's the use of striving to record amazing sounds if your monitors can't accurately reproduce the fruits of your labors?

If your recording environment is compromised by excessive audible hiss, the seek-and-destroy methods of analog recording still apply. Try to locate the source. Is it a noisy preamp? Fractured gain staging? A bad audio cable? You can either solve the problem or live with it, but remember, the digital medium often highlights sonic flaws.

STERILE INPUTS

When you start setting up microphones, maintaining tidy signals often means that less is more. A high-quality mic, well-placed in a good-sounding room, should be matched with short, premium cables and a clean preamp. Then, the signal should be routed directly to the recorder. Assigning signals to a subgroup adds another layer of electronics and the possibility of added noise.

But no matter how pristine your signal chain is, acoustic miking always is subject to unplanned environmental fanfares, which are eagerly documented by digital recording's extremely fine resolution. Beware of ambient noise, such as traffic, creeping into the background of a track. If the interstate highway runs through your back yard and room modification is not an option, you have two choices: Apply sonic bandages such as EQ and noise-gating, or record things that are less sensitive to the unwanted noise.

Taking the latter first, if you record a low-frequency track such as a bass guitar, the rumble of traffic may be acceptably masked by the source. Needless to say, loud rock 'n' roll drums, distorted guitars, and aggressive synth patches can cover a multitude of sins.

The "bandage" approach, however, requires putting on your sonic-sculptor hat and employing signal processing tricks. A highpass filter is the most common tool for reducing rumble, but take care not to thin out the overall sound. If

you have comprehensive EQ control (via your mixer input channels or an outboard graphic or parametric equalizer), cutting the signal below 100 Hz often diminishes low-end mud. You can also reduce audible hiss by rolling off some high frequencies. Noise-gating can clean up any unwanted sounds by shutting down the signal when the instrument is not playing. This approach works best on loud tracks, such as amplified guitars and blaring horn sections, that mask environmental noises during a performance.

Sounds input directly (without using a microphone) still are subject to unwanted noise from bass-guitar pickups and synthesizer and signal-processor outputs. Here, EQ and gating often are your surest weapons. To diminish pickup hum, have the bassist rotate until the quietest position is found, and ask that he or she play without moving from that spot.

OPTIMUM LEVELS

The digital medium also differs significantly from analog in the case of recording levels. The dynamic range of the analog medium is limited by increased tape hiss at low signal amplitudes and the recorder's headroom at high levels. Digital does not suffer from tape hiss on low-level material, but weak signals can exhibit quantization distortion. This distortion occurs when the digital medium attempts to convert a low-amplitude signal into finite values. Sometimes a puny level makes it difficult to get an accurate "description" of the incoming signal, and sample errors occur. Low-amplitude, high-frequency material is affected the most by quantization errors.

At high recording levels, digital offers no gradual increase in distortion as the headroom limit is approached (as analog often does). But going even a fraction over the headroom limit produces immediate and horrendous digital clipping. On some material, you might get away with the occasional clipping of a peak, but more than that is just plain ugly. Take this

At the 1976 Audio Engineering Society (AES) show, Thomas Stockham debuted his Soundstream Digital Tape Recorder by playing a digitally recorded and edited overture of an opera entitled *The Mother of Us All*. The opera session may have been the first practical digital field recording.

The Alesis ADAT was the first inexpensive digital multitrack tape deck to hit the marketplace, and it started a revolution. Suddenly, careful bedroom recordists could produce master tapes as sonically pristine as those recorded in large, megabucks studios.

into account when calibrating your mixer level to your recorder level: 0 VU on your mixer should be anywhere from 12 to 20 dB below the clip level of your digital recorder.

Where should you set your recording levels when recording digitally? Essentially, you are playing a game of brinkmanship, trying to see how close you can go to the edge of overload without going over. Signal peaks, such as those produced by a drummer's performance dynamics, can be deadly. I tend to err on the side of caution when setting recording levels. To my ears, a touch of quantization shenanigans caused by low recording levels is infinitely less annoying than digital clipping. If you're the nervous type, taming dynamics with a fast, transparent peak limiter often soothes "overload" tensions.

DIGITAL PARANOIA

If everything is done right, you should have a digital recording of startling clarity and detail. But when your finest aesthetic sense is thrilled by your achievement, should you rest on your laurels? Negative. It's time to get paranoid. Digital data can be very robust, but the storage medium may not be quite as tough, and the consequences can be dire.

If a digital tape acquires a crinkle—this happened to an Alesis ADAT S-VHS master on a recent project for which I played drums—or a disk drive fails, an entire cut (or even the whole master) may be rendered unplayable. I even had a recording savaged by the digital recording system itself. These impending tragedies always remind me of a computer-industry adage: Digital data does not exist until it is stored in at least two places. You always should have safety and backup copies of your digital masters.

Many hard-disk-based systems allow backup to DAT, which is an inexpensive way to buy some sonic security. (You can always erase and reuse DATs that store early backup versions.) I usually make a backup at the end of each hard-disk recording session. The only time I might risk

not making a backup is if I add one minor and easily reproducible overdub. But after each session in which I add new tracks, I make a safety copy, even if the process takes so long that it means leaving the system alone to make the backup while I do other things (like sleep).

If you own one Alesis ADAT or Tascam DA-88, it makes sense to find a "backup buddy" so you can link machines to make safety copies. Keep in mind that making a safety is worthwhile even if you can't stay in the digital domain. A safety copy with an extra generation of D/A and A/D conversion is better than no safety at all. Don't forget to use the best tape you can afford. Also, prepare your tapes for safe data storage by "breaking" the tape before recording. Simply fast-forward the tape to its end, then rewind it back to the beginning. This procedure helps reduce the likelihood of tape dropouts and other media-related artifacts.

A CD-R (recordable CD) deck is an excellent method of archiving finished products. The stability of CDs in comparison to digital tape or a hard disk more than justifies the cost of the medium. (Current stand-alone models start at approximately $3,500; the CDs themselves list at $30 each.)

CONCLUDING BITS

Digital recording is more accessible than anyone—except maybe Tom Stockham—could have envisioned twenty years ago. It's not really harder than analog recording; it just has some different characteristics and is less forgiving of errors. But once you develop a few of these basic good habits, great digital recordings will be yours. •

Hard-disk recording systems such as the Spectral Synthesis Digital Studio offer the powerful advantage of random access. This capability allows the user to easily edit bits and pieces of different tracks, or even performances, without touching the original recordings.

Digital multitrack tape recorders, such as the Tascam DA-88, offer inexpensive data storage, compared to hard-disk systems. Users can just let the tape run and record multiple takes of a work without fretting about available storage space.

3

Mixing
Your Demo

Producing the Ultimate Mix

AMERICA'S OBSESSION WITH FAMILY VALUES is all well and good for the moral majority, but what's in it for musicians? Well, I'll tell you: clarity. For better or for worse, liberal ideologies have obscured the definition of family. Society is confused. In short, it's a bad mix.

If the ebb and flow of social psychology could be mixed by someone like famous remix deity Bob Clearmountain, human strife might be little more than a memory. Clarity is essential for understanding, and a final mix needs coherence just as badly as humanity does.

Professional mix masters routinely mold disparate elements into an integrated, cohesive statement. Such clarity often marks the difference between a major-league master tape and a minor-league demo.

Producing pristine master tapes requires what I call "transparent mixing." It's a conceptual mindset that involves keeping all the elements of a recording sonically well-defined and subservient to the demands of the music. In other words, it means keeping a clean house so the neighbors can marvel over your new sofa.

STUDY HALL

What defines a good mix? Unfortunately, there are no absolute guidelines. Music is a wonderfully subjective medium, and arguments regarding a production's sonic quality—or lack thereof—can rage for hours. However, a *professional* mix is easy to identify: You can hear *everything*. The rhythm section punches through, the vocals are crisp, and even the sweetening (keyboard pads, psychoacoustic elements, counterpoint lines) is clear and well-articulated.

In addition, the ear is drawn to certain elements deemed by the artist or producer to be the work's focal points. On a pop record, these elements often are the lead vocal, rhythm section, and instrumental hook(s). Jazz producers typically highlight the soloist. In any case, a professional mixer ensures that the appropriate musical hooks are loud, clear, and unfettered by competing sonic elements.

Sadly, *unprofessional* mixes continue to be a hot commodity. My theory for this tragic state of affairs is that everybody believes they know how to mix a record. Give me a break! Unless you're a certified mixing genius, it takes years of practice, ear training, and intensive study

by Michael Molenda

before you can start churning out "hot" mixes. Some people never get it right. I've met a lot of talented fortysomething session monsters with years of studio experience who wouldn't dare mix their own demos. (At least they've acknowledged their limitations; few musicians seem willing to take a good look in the mirror.)

The first trick to producing transparent, professional mixes is to admit that you don't know everything. Instead of inflating your ego with unearned bravado, listen to classic and current recordings. Try to identify the elements that comprise a sharp, clean mix: What sounds are generally mixed up front; how many different instrumental and/or vocal "parts" are featured and what tonal ranges do they fill; and what is the basic sonic personality of the mix (a full tonal spectrum, predominant midrange frequencies, etc.)?

Once you've developed an ear for the components of professional masters, reference your own mixes to commercial CDs within your stylistic genre. Critically assess how your mixes stack up against professional products. If your tape sounds like pea soup compared to the latest Quincy Jones production, go back to study hall.

THE BIG PICTURE

Savvy producers conceptualize the final mix while the project still is being recorded. This means that a sonic ideal of the end product is always "on-line" in your brain throughout the entire recording process, from basic tracks to overdubs. Believe me, it's easier to record one "right" keyboard track than to sweat it out on the mix date trying to choose a

JOAN MARCUS

winner from fifteen different keyboard lines.

If you prepare supportive musical and sonic arrangements *before* committing a single sound to tape, the technical aspects of the mixing process—issues such as equalization tweaks and the relative

volume of instruments—should be almost automatic. Such preparation is rewarded by allowing you to concentrate on the more creative aspects of mixing, such as dimensional imaging (the placement of instruments within the stereo spectrum and tonal landscape), signal processing, and psychoacoustic translation (this is becoming more popular with ongoing advances in practical "3-D" audio reproduction). Obviously, it's also critical that you've carefully recorded every instrument in your production to yield optimal sonic quality. (Hopefully you've learned something from the preceeding chapters!)

All of this pre-production is important because the "fix it in the mix" scenario is a myth. The geniuses who can doctor a butchered master tape are rare and command fees commensurate with their miracle-making. In short, you can't afford them. But more importantly, you shouldn't need them. A little planning can save you hours of mixing frustration.

RECEPTACLES OF SOUND

An often-overlooked factor of transparent mixes is the recording medium. For example, an 8-track cassette ministudio may be technically unable to clearly reproduce scores of stacked instrumental tracks. The width of the cassette tape and the corresponding number of tape tracks, a slow tape speed (typically 3-3/4 ips), and track crosstalk usually don't add up

The inventor of multitrack recording, Les Paul (shown with his children, large and small), also was one mean mixer in his commercial heyday. His productions in the 1950s with then-wife Mary Ford sold millions of copies and thrilled audiences with layered vocals and echoing guitars.

The classic sound of the Beatles' *Sgt. Pepper's Lonely Hearts Club Band* was due, in part, to George Martin's (shown left, with Peter Townshend) miraculous expertise at submixing and bouncing tracks between two 4-track recorders.

to a transcendent audio spectrum. If you work with cassette ministudios, I recommend cutting tracks with relatively sparse instrumentation to ensure optimum sonic quality. The idea is to avoid overwhelming the recorder with more information than it can cleanly and accurately reproduce.

Digital mediums—both hard-disk and tape-based systems—don't suffer from the limitations of analog cassette formats, but that doesn't mean you can relax into a state of audio anarchy. For instance, it's critical that analog-experienced recordists disengage the habit of compensating for tape coloration. In the digital domain, what you put in is what you get out. Don't expect bass timbres to play back warmer than recorded (an often pleasing effect of analog tape coloration); they won't. If you want mammoth low end, construct the ultimate tone *before* you press Record.

Recording high frequencies also can be problematic for the inexperienced digital recordist. Once again, an analog habit can compromise your digital master. Many engineers boost treble frequencies when recording and mixing to compensate for the analog medium's generational sound loss. But if you crank the high end in the digital domain, the frequencies will remain cranked up during playback. (Remember: What goes in, comes out.) The result seldom is a pleasing—or even comfortable—listening experience. I've been able to identify musicians who recently have become proud owners of an Alesis ADAT by the fierce high end on their demo tapes.

Speaking of digital multitrack recorders, some engineers have discovered that a very slight high-end distortion appears when you start filling up tracks. It seems to be a progressive anomaly—not noticeable when a couple of tracks are recorded, barely noticeable when four or more tracks are recorded, and readily apparent when all eight tracks are filled—and may be one of the compromises inherent in modular digital recorders. This is another reason to go easy on the high-end tweaks when you are recording and mixing.

As you can see, getting intimate with your deck's "reproductive" capabilities is essential for producing optimum sonic environments. Before documenting your masterpieces on an unfamiliar or new recorder, I recommend running a few simple tests. Record insane amounts of bass and see how much bottom you can groove with before everything turns to mud. Likewise, track sizzling high-end information (cymbals, bright guitars, synth bells, etc.), and take note of where the sounds begin

Mathews' Mixing Mandates

Scott Mathews is an independent producer who has worked with artists as diverse as the divine Barbra Streisand and alternative folk-rock hero John Wesley Harding. I've always loved his mixes, because everything he does sounds like a hit single. All those indefinable elements that make up a great mix seem to be front-and-center in a Scott Mathews production. I asked Scott to write down a few guidelines ("I won't call them rules," he says, "because there are no such things in this biz.") that would help ensure competence, if not outright success, during a mix session. Here are his tips:

KNOW THE ARTIST. It's essential to ascertain where artists are coming from and where they want to go. Remember that the record you're mixing belongs to the artist, unless it's the 1960s and your name is Phil Spector.

DON'T DISREGARD ROUGH MIXES. More often than not, any rough mixes you've made throughout the recording process will have desirable qualities that should be considered at the final mix session. Roughs are fresh and intuitive, and often expose the raw truth of a performance. That's a rare and beautiful thing. Be careful not to "mix out" the passion by putting a magnifying glass over each and every track.

MIX WITH FRESH EARS. Morning mix sessions are optimum because your ears have not been abused by a typical day's activities. Ear fatigue is a real thing. After a few hours of near-field monitoring, the ears start compressing. You may feel like you're still ready to rock, but your hearing has turned to stone.

MONITOR AT REASONABLE LEVELS. Occasionally it's good to blast the speakers to check bass frequencies, but for the most part, soft playback levels tell the truth. (Also, it's hardly an insignificant consideration to protect your hearing.)

KNOW WHEN TO QUIT. When the fatigue factor reaches the point of diminishing returns, bail out. There's no sense in forcing yourself to finish something that probably will be remixed later when you've come to your senses. Also, take short breaks throughout the mix to rest your battered ears.

PUT THE MIX IN CONTEXT. Be sure to mix on familiar speakers to ensure critical listening. However, once the mix is finished, see if the sound translates well to the outside world. Check out the mix on different home stereo systems, portable "headphone" cassette players, car stereos, and boom boxes. After all, these are the mediums the public will use to hear your work.

BE OPEN TO REMIXING. Producers are in the unenviable position of keeping all factions happy with the end result, and everyone from label presidents to band managers has a vision of how a record should sound. It's a fact of life that producers must sometimes compromise their artistic visions to serve commerce. Rick Nelson was right when he sang "You've got to please yourself." Unfortunately, so was Bob Dylan when he wrote "You got to serve somebody."

smearing. Then, throw the kitchen sink on tape (or disk)—record drums and multiple guitar, keyboard, and vocal tracks up to the limit of your multitrack deck—and critically assess the clarity of your audio stew. Keep in mind that your tape recorder's electronic and mechanical health—as well as your engineering chops—also influences optimum sonic performance.

TRACK BY TRACK

The transparent mixer's primary mission (should he or she choose to accept it) is to put the track's money-maker in your face. This means that every mix decision is committed to turning the track into a supportive milieu for the lead vocal, solo instrument, or other musical hook. When you start playing with track levels and EQ environments, make sure that nothing interferes with the critical elements.

Only after you've identified a production's musical focal points should you risk obsessing (a little) over the individual components of your multitrack master. A transparent mix can only be achieved with slavish attention to detail. I've done countless remixes where most of the work was keeping tracks clean, rather than developing nifty sonic tricks or equalization tweaks. For those engineers who share my compulsion for neatness, here are some audio hygiene tips.

DISINFECTED DRUMS

One of the major causes of slaughtered drum tracks is the high-end wash produced by rapid-fire cymbal crashes. Some

GUIDO HARARI

drummers just *have* to smash a cymbal (or two) on every beat. This constant high-frequency overload not only is uncomfortable to listen to, but often smears the top end until it sounds like static.

Ideally, the producer should have helped the drummer develop a tight, sonically pleasing performance *before* the drums were recorded. Oh well. Unfortunately, most home studios lack the expensive equalizers that a pro studio or mastering facility would employ to tame the sizzle. An affordable option is to assign the individual drum tracks to a stereo submix and run the two channels through a stereo or dual de-esser. The de-esser often diminishes harsh treble frequencies to

It seems like there are few, if any, hit records that haven't been mixed by Bob Clearmountain (foreground, with pop star Bryan Adams). Clearmountain's critical ears arguably have molded the sound of 1980s and '90s pop music more than any other artist or producer.

the point where the basic mixer EQ can finish smoothing out the top end.

Snare drums often pose two problems: The player's dynamics can produce uneven tone (a hard thwack sounds quite different than an inadvertent rim shot or weak stroke), and the hi-hat, kick drum, and cymbals leaking through the snare mic make it difficult to add reverb without also affecting the other sounds. To produce a well-defined snare, I route the track through a noise gate to cut out everything except the actual snare hit. Then I send the signal to a compressor to even out the dynamics and produce an impact that's more "in your face." (It's important that the noise gate eradicate any stray cymbal crashes, as compression can raise their relative levels to the pain threshold.) The processed snare now will be isolated enough to cut through a thick mix and allow optimum reverb enhancement.

Kate Bush's theatrical, multilayered mixes of her own productions are virtual textbooks of fearless experimentation and evocative signal processing.

WHOLESOME BASS

I always compress the bass track to tame flabby dynamic levels, since low tones can fade into indistinct woofs if the player's picking or fingering technique is imprecise. A compression ratio of 2:1 or 4:1 at a threshold level of -10 dB usually tightens up the low end quite nicely. If I'm going for a "big bottom," I usually boost 100 Hz by 5 to 10 dB. However, I'll also cut the low mids, to keep too much bass information from muddying up the track. If a funkier bass tone is warranted, 100 Hz is cut by approximately 7 dB, and the mids are boosted to taste. Generally, if a noise gate is available, I'll use it to clean up the introduction, amp/preamp hiss, and instrumental breaks.

GERM-FREE GUITARS

The six-stringed demon probably is the preeminent nemesis of the transparent mixer. Electric guitars are temples of hum, hiss, and assorted audio belches. A noise gate is essential for shutting down ugly noises when the guitarist is not playing. (I detest hearing amp hiss in the background of rhythm section breakdowns or between arpeggiated chords.) Sometimes I'll compress an electric guitar signal to produce a "chunkier" sound. In these instances, hums and hisses often are accentuated. To combat the added noise, I'll cut a few dB off the bass frequencies to diminish the hum and insert a single-ended noise reduction device into the audio chain to tame the hiss.

Even the stately acoustic guitar can produce sympathetic harmonics that sabotage clarity. Unfortunately, there's not much you can do if an acoustic guitar isn't recorded well. To diminish muddiness without sacrificing too much of the quality of the instrument, cut the low-mids on your channel EQ. If the acoustic is one of the featured instruments in the mix and it still sounds "washy," consider re-recording it.

IMMACULATE SYNTHS

Just because the front panel says it's digital doesn't mean that the audio is clean. Sloppy samples and cheap output electronics are just two reasons why some keyboards exhibit audible hiss. To be safe, I usually employ a noise gate to kill

JEFF KATZ

Prince's mixes always seem to mess with recording conventions. For example, on one album the "Purple One" let acoustic kick drums ring out with harmonics, and then he mixed drum machine tracks completely dry on another. Each time, *his* way became the popular methodology.

any stray ugliness. This works fine when the synth isn't playing, but what about patches that seem to generate as much hiss as sound? If you have a single-ended noise reduction device, this is the time to use it. If not, try to cut the extreme high-frequencies on your channel EQ, or re-program the synth sound to tame the high end.

VISCERAL VOICES

Usually, the lead vocal is the most important element of a mix, and it helps if the sonic quality is worthy of its vaunted position. I always compress the vocal to get the voice more "up front." Compression also smoothes out performance dynamics. In many cases, a de-esser may be necessary to kill annoying sibilance. I usually try to maintain the integrity of a singer's tone by leaving the EQ flat, but

⦿ Mixed-Up Perceptions

A while back, a pal (who must remain nameless) produced a legendary country singer. When it came time to mix the first single, the record company president demanded five different mixes so that he could personally choose the best version for release. Of course, the producer—who had many successful records to his credit—wasn't about to let anybody but himself pick *the* mix.

So the president got his five mixes. However, every mix was exactly the same; not one note was changed between number one and number five. In addition, the producer sent a note saying: "Here are the requested five mixes. I know a hit record when I hear it, and number four is a smash. If you decide otherwise, you'll only have yourself to blame when the record flops!"

The next day, the president called and said, "Great work, babe, but I've chosen number five as the stronger mix."

The record bombed. However, because the producer knew which "version" was *really* the hit, he received a personal apology from the label president, who took full responsibility for choosing the flop. —*Scott Mathews* often the necessity of clarifying the voice within a dense track requires cutting some lows and boosting the mids at about 7.5 kHz.

Group background vocals also should be compressed to balance the dynamics of the individual singers. For "light" arrangements, an airy timbre can be produced by setting the compression ratio at 2:1 with a threshold of approximately -5 dB. To "toughen up" a big rock-'n'-roll chorus arrangement, increase the compression ratio to 10:1 and set the threshold at -10 dB. In both instances, the attack parameter should be in the median setting between slow and fast.

Don't forget that group sections will often cough, clear their throats, complain about the producer or engineer, and tell jokes when they're not singing. Protect your master tape's overall clarity by erasing the extraneous chatter before you mix, or by muting or gating the appropriate inputs during the mix. (I often receive demo tapes where I can hear someone coughing just before the chorus kicks in.)

HYGIENIC EFFECTS

Many engineers forget that signal processors can be brutally noisy. Once, an outside engineer complained that my studio was inundated with hiss. Confident that the system was about as sterile as an operating room, I traced the problem to a processor in the engineer's personal effects rack. When I muted the offending effects return, the silence was deafening. (Don't you love it when you can totally embarrass obnoxious "this-is-*your*-problem" types!) The moral of this story is obvious: The vigilant transparent mixer always puts noise gates on all effects returns.

THE SOFT FADE

Okay, we've spent hundreds of words expounding the concept of audio cleanliness; now prepare for one of those confusing little caveats: Some producers *like*

lip-smacking noises, horn-player breaths, and the whine, hum, and feedback of a guitar about to rip into a solo. They leave these sounds in the mix to promote a human factor, or maybe just because they sound cool. I've certainly been guilty of mixing in these so-called audio imperfec-

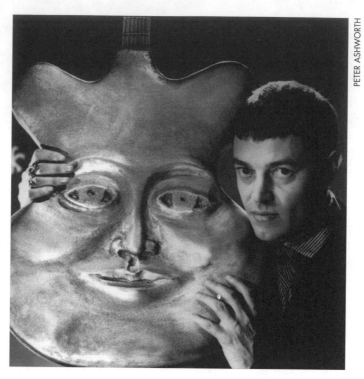

tions to capture a rough-and-ready vibe. Hey, you do whatever it takes to make the track bust loose.

However, the operative phrase here is "you do." An artistic choice is a conscious decision; unplanned noise is simply poor craft. A transparent sonic landscape puts the track's emphasis where it should be: on the performance. The public yearns to hear something special, like an incendiary sax solo or an impassioned vocal. They won't waste their time listening to audio muck. And while you can't send your master to a 12-step "clean-up" program any more than Bob Clearmountain can mix out the world's ills, a pristinely detailed transparent mix can make your productions shine. •

Bill Nelson, ex-Be Bop Deluxe guitar idol and godfather of "do-it-yourself" record production, consistently produces slamming mixes with low-tech gear. His reverential cult popularity—and occasional successes in dance clubs and on alternative radio stations—should be an inspiration to home recordists.

Reflecting on Reverb

BACK WHEN PHIL SPECTOR INVENTED THE "WALL OF SOUND," outboard reverb units consisted of long springs, heavy plates, and specially designed acoustic chambers. Obviously, few of today's personal recording studios have the space to accommodate these signal-processing monsters from the past.

But unlike recording engineers (who are still debating analog vs. digital audio), reverb lovers can embrace the digital age without reservation. Thanks to the microchip, a smorgasbord of acoustic environments can fit into a 19-inch rackspace. Effectively using this bounty of easily accessible acoustical environments is another matter; heavy-handed application of reverb can turn a well-recorded track into runny lasagna.

We Are Family

One of the major mixing applications for reverb is putting diverse elements into a common acoustical environment. An engineer often designates a particular unit—whether it's a personal favorite, the best box available, or a device noted for sonic excellence—as the "master" reverb. This overall reverb, which often is set to a medium or large room (or plate) with a decay time somewhere between 1.5 to 2.5 seconds, is used to process, in varying amounts, each instrument in the mix.

In effect, the master reverb gives the track an illusion of cohesiveness: A syn-thesizer without a natural (or internally processed) environment can sound like it was recorded in the same room as an electric guitar. The master reverb can bestow identical acoustic qualities upon each instrument, fooling the ear into believing the "band" played together. Multi-track sessions often record instruments at different times and in diverse acoustical environments, so employing a master reverb can make a track sound more organic.

Hitting the Tracks

While developing a master reverb is the most *organic* method of environmental control, it isn't the only way to spice up tracks, or even always the most appropriate. Some engineers match individual reverb programs to specific instruments, then mix the processed tracks in a common "room" created with a master reverb. Other engineers couldn't care less about a cohesive environment and purposefully create diverse programs that highlight particular sounds and instruments. If you want to break up the band (sonically speaking), here are some specific reverb applications and ideas.

by Neal Brighton

Drums

Although less fashionable today, gated reverb has been a popular percussion enhancement for years. In the past, a gated reverb sound was produced by sending the reverb returns (or outputs) into a noise gate and setting the threshold and release parameters to abruptly snap off the reverb decay. Now, almost every multi-effects device offers this sound as a factory preset. A short decay "tail" can add more punch to snare tracks, although the resulting effect is considered by some to be rather clichéd. Playing with the gated reverb's room size and decay time can produce anything from pistol-shot slap-backs (cool on snares) to bizarre "percussive" reverb tails (very tricky on toms).

sound source and reflective surfaces. If preliminary reflections or reverberation anticipate the direct percussion sound, you may end up with some weird, disorienting timing anomalies.

GUITARS

When it comes to putting reverb on guitars, almost anything goes. Just make sure the decay time isn't so long that it washes out the track—a common mixing problem. If you really want ripping guitar tracks, critically assess if reverb treatment is necessary. A typical miked amplifier usually

Some guitar effects processors, such as the Alesis QuadraVerb GT, offer flexible reverb parameters and can do double duty in the home studio.

If you want punchy tracks but can't stomach gated-reverb effects, try a short decay on a moderately large room or plate program. This big/short combo maximizes the impact of the drum without allowing a long decay to obscure other instruments. On a recent remix project, the drums (kick, snare, hi-hat, three toms, and four cymbals) were submixed to two tracks by the original engineer to free up space for more instrumental parts. It was obvious at mixdown that the stereo drum tracks were pretty limp compared to the rest of the mix. Employing the big/short reverb energized the drum tracks without adding an obnoxious reverb decay to the hi-hat and cymbals. Minimal effort rendered the drum sound "naturally" punchy and saved the mix.

When constructing reverb environments, keep in mind that plate programs often accentuate the highs, while rooms tend to exhibit warmer timbres. Also, take care with the amount and time of early reflections, diffusion, and pre-delay. These parameters provide aural clues that help indicate not only room size, but where the listener is sitting relative to the

produces suitable ambience (depending on the room in which the guitar was recorded); if further treated with a guitarist's favorite effects processor, the guitar signal may already be overprocessed. Depending on the mix and performance style, adding more reverb can actually *diminish* the power of the guitar.

My rule of thumb is to start with a completely dry track. If the guitars burn, leave them alone. If not, sneak some reverb in until you're happy, then quit while you're ahead. It's always better to use less reverb than you think you need.

KEYBOARDS

Except for lush string programs, few synths and sampler tracks survive being washed in large reverbs. The overwhelming ambience reduces most sounds to audio mush. But electronic instruments often benefit from a little extra substance. One of my tricks for fattening up synth tracks involves running the signal into a reverb unit that has a large room setting with a short decay time. Then I route the output of this reverb into *another* reverb unit set with a medium plate and a long decay. The first reverb setting emulates the acoustics that would have existed if the sound source were miked, and the second reverb blends the synth into the overall mix. Be sure to adjust the wet/dry mix of the second reverb (or the effects-return levels, if you're routing the outputs of both units into your mixer) to prevent the long decay from compromising overall clarity.

Vocals

The lead vocal track often screams for reverb. Actually, the lead *vocalist* often screams for reverb. And he or she always demands tons more than is appropriate. Unfortunately, a voice submerged under a sea of reverb only serves to sink your mix. Because the vocal often is the prime element of a track, you must stop reverb overkill by any means necessary. A subtly processed voice punches out from the track; a reverb-doused mess usually gets lost in the wash.

If you insist on using a reverb with a long decay, try holding back on the effects-return level. A barely audible reverb wash provides a nice background ambience without overwhelming the track. And don't forget that adjusting a short reverb's pre-delay can make a relatively dry vocal treatment sound "wet": You simply move the onset of reverb closer to the direct signal (voice). In addition, keep in mind that every voice has a different quality and timbre, so audition plate and room reverbs until you find the program that works best.

Cleaning House

One of the major causes of compromised sound in effects devices is failure to maximize the signal input. If you want to get more reverb out of your box, don't instantly crank up the output; such a maneuver only increases your chances of dumping hiss into a clean mix. First, make sure the signal input level of the unit is as hot as it can get without distorting, *then* boost your output to the desired level. This simple technique maximizes your signal-to-noise ceiling.

It also pays to solo your reverb returns to check noise levels. Many low- and mid-priced processors exhibit some level of au-

dible hiss, so I always put a noise gate on the effect returns. The gate ensures that residual noise is silenced when no signal is running through the reverb unit. Take care to set the gate's threshold and release parameters so that the reverb can decay completely. Some processors have internal EQ, and you always can run your effects returns into a mixer channel for equalization purposes, so there is almost no excuse for muddy reverb. I usually cut some bass frequencies to enhance clarity.

A little-known problem is that using two or more models of the same reverb unit can cause signal-phasing. Try reversing the left and right outputs of each unit if you notice that your mids and highs are compromised.

Quick Delay

Well, there you have it. Reverb can make your mix sound larger than life, or it can flush clarity down the audio drain. If you employ reverb in a mix, don't forget that the effect plays as much a part in the overall sound as the instrument you are processing.

Ultimately, all the elements of a track influence the final sonic mix. So don't let that paranoid vocalist talk you into decorating his or her voice with the "Grand Canyon" reverb program. (This warning goes double if *you* are the vocalist.) And remember, keeping your tracks clean doesn't mean you can't have fun. Once I've maximized my signal levels, I toss the manuals into a drawer and start goofing with every reverb parameter I can get my hands on. •

Simple but powerful units such as Lexicon's LXP-1 deliver smooth ambience and intuitive parameter control.

Deploying Delay

FROM THE WHISPER OF A BUTTER-FLY'S WINGS beating in the air to the loudest crescendo of a symphony orchestra, all audio can be described by two parameters: amplitude and time. In essence, the terms we use to describe music—pitch, timbre, rhythm, melody, and so on—define variations in these parameters.

We perceive changes in amplitude because our ears are sensitive to how air moves. The tiny twitches of air molecules against our eardrums tell us the location and nature of people and objects in our environment. Acoustically, we deal with time in day-to-day life in the form of acoustic echoes. These delays are so much a part of aural perception that we seldom notice them, yet they form much of the basis of our ability to locate and identify sounds.

The upshot of all this is that when we apply delay in recording and performance, we are controlling amplitude and time at an extremely basic level. Whether creating audio illusions not possible in any real acoustic space or trying to simulate a specific acoustic environment accurately, delay is a powerful tool for playing with a listener's perception.

How time delay affects sound depends on the delay time itself, along with the amplitude and frequency content of the delayed signal as compared to the original. The presence of any other delays and any differences between the sounds that arrive at the left and right ears also are critical factors.

The sonic characteristics of different delays usually are related to specific time ranges (**Fig. 1**). In reality, these ranges cannot be defined so precisely. In particular, at short delay times the effect is vastly different for stereo and mono signals. With that caveat in mind, here are some typical effects correlated to approximate delay times.

STEREO IMAGE EFFECTS
0 TO 5 MILLISECONDS

Delay times of less than a couple of milliseconds primarily affect imaging, but only when the original signal predominates in one ear and the delayed signal predominates in the other. When heard over headphones, the sonic image tilts strongly to the ear receiving the non-delayed signal. (This happens because our auditory system uses the difference in path length from one ear to the other as a key cue in determining lateral direction of sound in nature.)

Over loudspeakers, the effect is less distinct, due to the blending of sound from each speaker with reflected sound from the listening environment. Generally, you'll hear a spread of the stereo image that changes as you turn your head or change position. Small time delays between channels can help build separations between tracks in a sonically cluttered production. To embed imaging information in the tracks, use small delays

by Gary Hall

of differing values for different tracks, and alternate which speaker channel receives the non-delayed signal (**Fig. 2**). Be careful when applying this technique, because effects that sound subtle over loudspeakers can be excessive when monitored on headphones.

SEPARATION EFFECTS
10 TO 35 MILLISECONDS

Setting delay levels and pans so that environmental reflections are not suggested creates the effect of a separate but equal sound source. The principle behind doubling is that the ear will treat the delayed signal as another sound source, because the two occur at different times. However, in practice, a simple delay is not enough to create a credible doubling effect; introducing small pitch shifts by altering the delay time produces a more realistic effect. Periodic LFO-induced shifts are less convincing than random shifts, but not if the random changes occur too quickly. Also, one of the traditional ways of generating random shifts—the sample-and-hold waveform—often changes too abruptly to be usable. It's better to use a smoothed sample-and-hold, which acts more like a triangle-wave LFO whose speed varies randomly within a certain range.

Using a pitch shifter tuned at or very near unity creates a very convincing illusion of two independent sources if you pan the unshifted and shifted signals to opposite stereo channels. (Some pitch shifters do not have a true unity, other than bypass.) When the tuning is placed very close to unity, the result is a kind of random phase modulation.

In theory, chorusing creates the sound of a large number of sources playing identical lines *en ensemble*. In reality, chorusing can be a wonderful means of enriching a sound that simulates, rather than duplicates, the ensemble effect. The line between doubling and chorusing is a blurry one, and sometimes it seems that any doubling setting that is too pronounced to be realistic is called "chorusing."

SLAP ECHO
50 TO 150 MILLISECONDS

In this range, a sound's delayed repeat is very distinct from the original. However, sounds with very slow attacks and de-

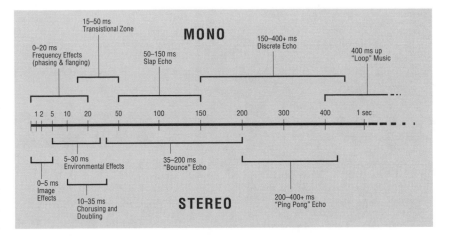

FIG. 1
The continuum of delay effects in mono and stereo.

cays may tend to blend. (Such sounds often obscure many of the effects we are talking about, because the ear usually uses the sounds' initial transients to correlate the direct and delayed sounds.)

In mono, the effect is that of a fast stutter or a repeat of the sound. Depending on the characteristics of the sound and the relationship between the levels, slap echo also may "fatten" the sound, or broaden the attack. In stereo, a "ricochet" effect occurs, which may cause listeners to jerk their attention from the undelayed to the delayed speaker. To accentuate this effect, route the delayed signal through a bandpass filter to cut the high and low end, feed the signal to a reverb unit, and delay one channel of the reverb output (the one opposite the "dry" version of the delayed sound) by 50 to 100 milliseconds.

DISCRETE ECHO EFFECTS
150 TO 400 MILLISECONDS

In this range—the classic "Echoplex" zone—delayed sounds are clearly and fully distinct from the original and are heard as separate repetitions. (Is there a guitarist or vocalist who is not thrilled to hear the repeat, repeat, repeat of their licks fading into the air?)

Often it is important to select delay times that work rhythmically with the music. For some musical styles, it's best if delay times synchronize with the beat. You can figure out a complementary delay time by using the following equation: Delay time in milliseconds = 60,000 ÷ tempo in beats per minute (bpm).

In other instances, you may want delays that do not correspond to the beat. These tend to "cut across" the dominant

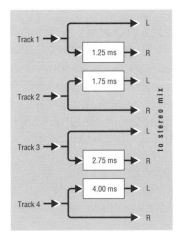

FIG. 2
Using delays to add imaging to a stereo mix. Note the use of different delay times and the alternation of which channel precedes the other.

CHESTER SIMPSON

beat and gain their power from their very lack of an easily discernible relationship to the main beat.

It is easy to overuse echo, so exercise caution; crowding too many repeating delays into a mix turns it into an indistinct wash. Controlling the signal going to the delay, either with effects sends at a mixing console or with foot pedals, can regulate the amount of echo. This also lets you do tricks such as adding echoes selectively (just to the tail ends of phrases, for example) by feeding only the target signal into the delay line. When you pull back on the input level, the echoes will continue but no subsequent sound will be processed.

DELAY LOOPS
400 MILLISECONDS AND UP

When delays become long enough to equal musical bars, phrases, and sections, we get into an area that some call loop music. Guitarist Robert Fripp popularized this effect by constructing sonic symphonies of undulating guitar lines (and sounds) and dubbing them "Frippertronics." Other practitioners of loop music include David Torn, Brian Eno, Steve Tibbetts, and Andy Summers. Loop music is virtually a subculture unto itself.

DELAYING THE CONSEQUENCES

As you experiment with delay, use your ears and your mind together. Consider the nature of the sounds themselves and the music in which you use them. No signal processing occurs in a vacuum; there always is a rich interaction of one sound with another. Use these interactions to your own advantage, and you'll achieve sounds that can leap out and grab the listener's attention. •

Robert Fripp (far left) popularized his "Frippertronics" by creating sonic symphonies *sans* band.

More Tricks for Delay Disciples

FAUX STEREO. One of the simplest delay tricks involves transforming a monaural signal into a pseudo-stereo image. This application is particularly valuable if you're limited to four or eight tape tracks. A mono signal can be "cloned" through a delay processor, returned on a free input module or effects return, and panned opposite the original tape track. *Voila*, faux stereo! I usually start with the delay time at 10 ms to produce a "snapshot" copy of the original track. You can widen the spectrum a little by adjusting the delay time to between 30 and 50 ms.

VOCAL SLAPBACK. Everyone knows about cowabunga vocal ec-ec-echoes, but delay also can be used subtly to add depth to a voice. A 75-millisecond setting with no repeats (or feedback) delivers a classic slapback effect. Panning the delayed or slapback signal a little to the right or left of the original (centered) vocal helps clarify the effect. Sometimes it may be appropriate to have some fun by panning the original vocal full left and the delayed signal full right. Obviously, the delayed signal has to sound as clear as the actual vocal for this trick to work. The ragged resolution of inexpensive, guitar-oriented processors usually betrays the illusion.

THE NEVER-ENDING VOCAL ECHO. Long delays with moderate repeats provide the foundation of my favorite trick for adding dimension to a predominantly dry vocal. Set the delay unit to approximately 375 milliseconds, with ten to fifteen repeats; don't forget to match the tempo of the repeats to the song. Fade this percolating chorus of echoes far below the level of the original vocal track. At first listen, the voice may appear almost completely dry. Certain phrases, however, should betray the delay effect and help pull the listener into the song.

Some producers mix the multiple repeats as loud (or louder) than the lead vocal to add importance to selected lyrical phrases. This application is an old dub (Jamaican club music) standard and has been adopted by the current generation of rap, techno, and other dance-oriented artists.

AURAL GHOSTS. Another of my favorite tricks is using delay to retard the onset of a reverb. Basically, you send the selected tape track into the delay unit and route the delayed signal into a reverb. The actual delayed signal is not audible, only the delayed reverb. The delay unit is set to zero feedback because you just want the signal to arrive at the reverb unit a few milliseconds "late." How late the delayed signal triggers the reverb effect is up to you. I typically choose a rather languid timing of 250 to 500 ms, depending on the tempo and feel of the track. The reverb unit—again, depending on the atmosphere you're trying to achieve—should have a large or medium room setting, with a long decay time.

At its best, this application produces a spooky effect that sounds great on lead vocals or slow, melodic solos. (The delay ping-pongs caused by high-speed soloing usually are too intense for most uses.) On vocals, the lyrics seem to "shadow" the lead vocal: The lush reverb softly repeats the words a few milliseconds after the actual vocal track is heard. I find that this effect is more sensual than the chopped repeats produced by pure echo. Some multi-effects processors allow you to place a delay before a reverb in an algorithm, so this ghosting effect often can be accomplished with one box.—*Michael Molenda*

Prescriptions for Pitch Shifting

BACK IN THE 1970S, real-time pitch shifters were so exotic that the Eventide Harmonizer was the only reasonable choice. Unfortunately, these beauties weren't cheap, and their fidelity often left something to be desired. Since then, vigorous research and development has improved the capabilities and quality of pitch shifters while lowering their cost. Now these tools are available to practically everyone.

Isn't it a shame, then, that the widespread conception of pitch shifting remains narrow and unclear? Pitch shifting may be harder to master than basic reverb applications, but it's not a dark secret. Anyone can become one of the *cognoscenti,* reveling in the magic spells required to convince friends of your signal-processing genius, in just the few minutes it takes to read this chapter.

CORRECTNESS COUNTS

There are three general applications for pitch shifting: correction, enhancement, and special effects. Easy correction of off-pitch recordings became possible with the advent of context-sensitive, a.k.a. "intelligent," pitch shifters in the mid-1980s. Thanks to these devices, good (or even great) performances don't have to be ruined by a few bad notes. For example, you can copy a pitch-compromised vocal track onto a fresh track, run the original track through a pitch shifter adjusted to compensate for the bad notes, and punch the "fixed" notes into the copy track (**Fig. 1**). When completed, the copy track becomes a composite of original and corrected performances. In other words, the composite track is now an assemblage of "pitch-perfect" takes.

Occasionally, a sound may be off-pitch by a consistent amount, as if the tape deck were running off-speed when the track was recorded. This problem can be corrected easily by running the offending track through a pitch shifter tuned to the desired reference pitch. Obviously, only the corrected version should be audible during mixdown.

A bigger problem is a track with random pitch inaccuracies. The culprit may have been uneven tape speed in the original recorder (often the result of worn capstans or rollers) or a sloppy performance. Fortunately, context-sensitive pitch shifters can "pitch-quantize" an entire performance. Fixing wobbly pitches requires routing the track through a context-sensitive pitch shifter set to correct all notes within a defined range. The device automatically "auditions" every note and corrects the slackers.

by Larry the O

This type of processing often salvages a wide variety of errors, but beware: The action of even the best pitch shifters can become audible when a majority of the notes are corrected. Heavy-handed pitch correction usually works best on tracks that are not highlighted in the mix. However, if you must apply such high levels of correction to a featured track—such as a lead vocal—pitch-shifting artifacts probably are not your greatest worry!

Oddly, sometimes more can be less in pitch correction. A subtle approach to saving a track with pitch problems is a trick I call *pitch concealment.* This application does not correct the pitch, but attempts to make the problem less obvious to the listener. Such tonal camouflage is accomplished by exploiting chorusing effects that fool the ear into averaging the pitch of multiple sources.

Electronic chorusing effects are based largely on small, variable amounts of pitch shifting. A good, thick chorus—preferably with more than two voices—can smear pitch perception enough to hide many intonation problems. The key tweaks are the depth of chorusing and the mix between the chorused and original signals (which usually needs to be nearly equal for the technique to work).

Although chorus speed is important, a more crucial consideration is the nature of the modulation creating the chorusing effect. Ideally, all voices should not be chorused identically. Examples of this effect are the random modulation found in the Lexicon 224X and LXP-1 chorus programs and the ability of devices such as the DigiTech IPS-33B and Eventide Ultra-Harmonizer to apply independent modulation to the pitch and/or delay time of their voices.

Another pitch-concealment application involves mixing enough of a pitch-corrected track with a pitch-compromised track to make the combined sound "feel" on-pitch. This method helped me salvage a performance where the vocalist's intonation was slightly sharp throughout an entire song.

ENHANCING THE EXPERIENCE

The greatest value of pitch shifting often is signal enhancement: Pitch shifters can be used to thicken a sound, spread it into stereo, add depth or brightness, or animate it.

The simplest method of thickening or doubling a vocal or other track—outside

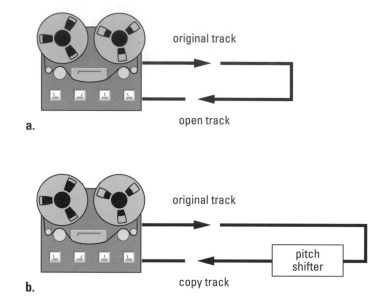

a.

original track

open track

b.

original track

pitch shifter

copy track

FIG. 1
Using a pitch shifter to correct bad notes in an otherwise good performance: (a) Copy the pitch-compromised track to an open track. Then (b) route the original track into a pitch shifter adjusted to correct the pitch problem, and punch the corrected note into the copy track. Correct one note at a time, repeating the procedure as needed.

of having the singer replicate the performance on a separate track—is to use 15 to 30 milliseconds of delay to "clone" the signal onto an effects return (or an available input module). Modulating the delay improves the illusion, but shifting the pitch by a few cents improves it even more. If your processor offers more than one voice of pitch shifting, set the voices to complementary amounts (+5 cents and -5 cents, for example). This doubling technique also helps construct exceptionally fat bass tracks. Remember, enhancement usually requires subtlety, so go light on the amount of pitch shift, modulation, and wet/dry mix.

To spread a mono track into stereo, simply pan the pitch-shifted voice(s) away from the original. For lead vocals, I usually use complementary shifts (*sans* modulation), panned right and left, with the original source in the middle. Varying the degree of panning changes the apparent width of the image. It's also fun to add very short amounts of modulated delay (between 5 to 10 ms) to the pitch-shifted sound to destabilize the stereo imaging: The source appears to float around the stereo field. I call this technique "animating" the source, and it's one of my favorite tricks.

Pitch shifting also can be used to add depth or brightness to drum tracks. I tune my snare drum very high, but for some rock mixes it needs a little more "beef." In these cases, I shift the snare down (sometimes as much as a few semitones), roll off the high EQ, and carefully mix the pitch-shifted snare with the original. Now I have the snap of the original with the body of a deeper snare.

Conversely, a flat, "cereal-box" snare can be made snappier by mixing in an up-shifted copy. But be careful: The ear hears imperfections in higher components more clearly than in lower ones. Toms and kick drums also can benefit from judicious pitch enhancement. However, keep in mind that any sound leaking into the drum mics will be pitch-enhanced as well. I often employ a noise gate on the send to the pitch shifter. Careful gating usually ensures that only the desired source sound is processed.

SHIFTING INTO OVERDRIVE

Producing special effects can be the most enjoyable application of pitch shifting. The most obvious trick is using radical pitch shifts on a voice to produce "helium" (up-shift) or "monster" (downshift) effects. But even more wildness awaits the fearless. For example, context-sensitive shifters can generate harmonies within a specified tonality; some even allow you to specify the amount of shift for each note of the scale. I once used this function to transform a solo violin into a demented string section. Again, keep in mind that harmonies *above* the original are usually more detectable as "phonies" than harmonies below.

But wait, there's more! Adding substantial delay to the shifted voices produces great echo/arpeggiation effects. You can get even crazier by adding some regeneration (feedback). A pitch shift of a minor third, with a few hundred milliseconds of delay and some feedback, can take a single note and turn it into an upwardly spiraling, arpeggiated diminished chord. Now try one voice of upshift and one voice of downshift, both with feedback. Are we unintelligible yet?

Besides being fun, these tricks often are employed by film sound designers to wrench fantastic sound effects from commonplace objects: A match being struck becomes a supernova explosion; a sink full of water is transformed into a raging ocean; and a buzzsaw metamorphosizes into the 700-foot killer mosquito from Planet X.

PITCHED OUT

As with all digital processors, overloading a pitch shifter's input produces truly ugly sounds. Unfortunately (for reasons that remain unclear to me), some pitch shifters are unusually susceptible to overload. I often insert a compressor before the send to the pitch shifter to avoid nuking the input level. In the future, I'd love to see manufacturers include onboard analog limiting on the inputs to *all* digital processors. Keep in mind that the greater the pitch shift, the more audible the artifacts.

Also, don't forget that non-real-time pitch shifting, such as that found on samplers and many digital audio workstations,

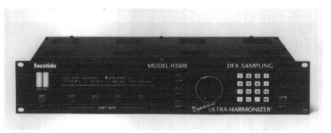

In the 1970s, Eventide produced one of the first practical real-time pitch shifters. A recent update to the lineage, the H3500 Ultra-Harmonizer, offers sampling in its multi-effects menu.

can be used for some of the applications I've discussed, as well as many others.

In my experience, pitch shifters can broaden the sonic palette more than any other type of processing except reverb. They can be utilitarian one second and lunatic the next. As always, the real limitations are only your imagination and taste.   •

Dynamics Processing

DYNAMICS PROCESSORS—limiters, compressors, expanders, and noise gates—are the most misunderstood of all signal processors. And they can be touchy—mishandle a compressor and it'll squash the life from a good recording. But don't be scared. Once you understand them, dynamics processors can make the difference between a good recording and a great one. And they're really not difficult to use.

Dynamics processors alter the *dynamic range* of audio signals by changing the relationship of the loud parts to the soft parts, dramatically affecting how a sound is recorded and reproduced. Dynamic range is a ratio of the amplitude difference between the softest and loudest sound that a musical instrument can produce. Dynamically speaking, not all sounds are created equal. A symphony orchestra is capable of fantastic dynamic range; typically more than 70 decibels between its quietest and loudest levels. The harpsichord, however, registers a smaller dynamic range, because there isn't much of a difference in amplitude between a soft touch and a forceful pluck.

Compressors and limiters are the best-known dynamics processors, and are used to *reduce* a signal's dynamic range. On the other side are expanders and gates, which *increase* dynamic range. When should these tools be used? How do they differ? Let's find out.

COMPRESSORS

Vocalists are capable of tremendous dynamic range. That's great, but it's difficult to find optimum recording levels when a singer constantly throws screams and whispers at you. Riding the faders up and down to track signal levels is madness; you'll never react fast enough to catch sudden peaks.

A compressor frees you from "fader riding" by acting as a gain control. The user specifies an input threshold, below which signals pass through unaffected. However, when signals rise *above* the threshold, the compressor kicks in and reduces their level. A compressor helps an engineer set an average recording level between high- and low-amplitude signals (**Figs. 1** and **2**). The result is consistent, more professional tracks, unmolested by tape saturation or the hiss produced by low recording levels.

A common misconception is that compressors make loud passages quieter and quiet *by Brent Hurtig* passages louder. Here's what really happens: Because loud signals are reduced, the dynamic range between loud and quiet passages is also reduced. The quiet passages *seem* louder, even though they're not processed.

LIMITERS

Limiting is an extreme form of compression: Levels that exceed the set threshold

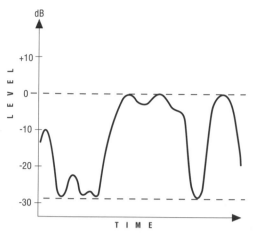

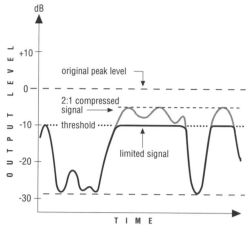

FIG. 1 (far left)
The amplitude envelope
of an unprocessed audio
signal.

FIG. 2
The same signal envelope,
illustrating compression at a
2:1 ratio and limiting. The
threshold in each case is set
at 10 dB below the
uncompressed peak.

are effectively stopped from getting any louder. A good limiter can let you set an *absolute* maximum signal level.

Limiters typically are used as safety devices. For example, anyone who has played live knows it's easy to produce spontaneous Roger Daltrey-style vocal shrieks (or feedback loops, or drum ka-ka-pows) capable of destroying a speaker. To prevent these mishaps, most professional sound systems are equipped with limiters to "catch" surprise signal peaks.

In the studio, however, limiters are used to prevent overloading the recorder so that distorted signals are not printed to tape (or allowed to munch the bits on your hard disk). Although vocals and drums are the main offenders, any source with a quick, unpredictably loud attack is a candidate for a "safety limit."

DUCKERS AND DE-ESSERS

Duckers and de-essers are variants of the basic compressor, and perform very specific—and extremely useful—tasks. Duckers often are used in broadcast advertising (jingles, voice-overs, etc.) to automatically reduce the volume of the music bed when an announcer is speaking. Basically, a ducker is a compressor controlled by a *side-chain* input. The music bed is put through the normal compressor input(s), and the announcer's voice is routed to the side-chain input. When the level of the announcer's voice exceeds the threshold set by the user, the level of the music is reduced in proportion to the level of the voice.

De-essing is a frequency-dependent dynamics process that also is based on a side-chain trigger. De-essers are indispensible for taming the annoying sibilants produced by some singers during recording. (Sibilants are those searing "sss," "sshhh," and "tsch" sounds that can compromise a good vocal performance.)

For de-essing, an EQ (parametric or graphic) is connected to the compressor's side-chain input. Now that the EQ'd signal is controlling the compressor—just as the level of an announcer's voice triggers ducking—the engineer simply boosts the sibilant frequencies (typically

● The Dynamic Control Panel

THRESHOLD. Determines the level at which processing kicks in. With compressors and limiters, signals that cross *above* the threshold level get processed; with expanders and gates, only signals *below* the threshold are processed.

RATIO. Refers to the ratio between a change in input level and the corresponding change in output. Ratio range depends upon the job at hand. Compression calls for ratios of 2:1 to 10:1. Limiting implies very high compression ratios of 10:1, 20:1, or even ∞:1. For expanders, opposite ratios are the way to think: A 3:1 ratio setting on the box really should be thought of as a 1:3 setting, since a 1 dB drop in input level will be expanded to a 3 dB drop in output level once the signal drops below threshold.

ATTACK AND RELEASE. The attack control determines how quickly—from milliseconds to a full second or longer—processing kicks in once a signal has crossed the set threshold. A release control lets you set how much time passes before the processing stops, once the signal crosses back under (or over, in the case of an expander or gate) the threshold. Quick releases are best for peak control, and moderate or longer release times are better for more natural-sounding processing.

GAIN-REDUCTION METER. Usually calibrated in decibels (dB), this meter shows how much processing takes place once signals cross the threshold.

SIDE-CHAIN INPUT. Sometimes referred to as "Key In," this input engages the external side-chain return so that external signals control the VCA (see the other sidebar, "VCAs and Side-Chains").

SLAVE. Dual-channel processors usually sport a slave switch which puts the "slave" channel (usually the right channel, or channel two) under the complete control of the "master channel" (usually the left channel, or channel one).

between 3 kHz and 8 kHz) so that the compressor reacts to them more aggressively than the rest of the tonal spectrum. The result is a smooth attenuation of sibilants. There also are dedicated de-essers available that include some type of onboard EQ and a side-chain.

EXPANDERS

When you need to increase dynamic range, call in an expander. In over-simplified terms, an expander is like a backwards compressor: Expansion kicks in when a signal drops *below* a user-set threshold, resulting in a gradual reduction of gain.

There are three main uses for an expander: Restoring dynamic range to "squashed" or over-compressed signals; reducing low-level background noises such as hiss, tape crosstalk, and microphone bleed (you always can count on rhythm track leakage from the headphones into vocal mics); and cutting unwanted decay from a signal.

NOISE GATES

Just as limiting is a form of maximum compression, noise-gating is expansion taken to its most extreme. When a signal drops below the set threshold, its level is not just reduced, but shut off completely. Only signals that rise above the threshold can "open" the gate and become audible.

Gates are perfect for eliminating hum and buzz when an instrument is not playing. Electric guitars, for instance, are notorious noisemakers; a gate can shut down the unwanted cacophony during silent passages. Gates also can be used to shut out background noise, such as lip-smacks and page-turning, from miked sources. The key to success, as with any dynamics processor, is careful adjustment. An improper setting can "clip" the attack from lyrical phrases or cause audible "stuttering" if a signal wavers around the threshold level.

PRACTICAL PROCESSING

Well, now that you know the basics about how dynamics processors work, what can you *do* with these devices? Plenty! Here are some favorite "tricks of the trade" that engineers have used on countless productions. This list of applications is not comprehensive—signal processing of any type is limited only by the user's imagination and ingenuity—but should get you excited about the ultimate power of dynamics processing.

Smooth Vocals. This classic vocal compression is very subtle and even. Set your compression ratio anywhere between 3:1 and 5:1 (adjust to taste, of course), with a threshold level of 2 dB to 6 dB below the peak. The attack time should be moderately fast, and the release time slow. If excessive peaks ruin the effect, run the source into a limiter first (using fast attack and release times) and adjust the threshold to limit troublesome peaks.

Breathy Vocals. To create whispery, in-your-face vocals, set your compression ratio between 5:1 and 10:1, with a threshold level of 6 dB to 20 dB below the peak. Attack time should be very fast, with a moderate release time. The effect is better articulated when a bit of reverb is used for additional processing. Beware: Achieving this effect requires compression so intense that breaths, lip-smacks, and other background noise will seem incredibly loud. A pop filter is recommended while recording.

Sustained Bass. A smooth, legato bass sound can be achieved by setting your compression ratio between 3:1 and 6:1, with a threshold level 2 dB to 9 dB below the peak. The attack time should be very fast, release time moderate to slow. After the instrument's initial attack, sustained notes will increase in gain, resulting in a sensual sustain. The length of the sustain can be modified by adjusting the threshold and attack time parameters.

Drums O' Doom. The classic Phil Collins rumble employs a compressor to brutally squash the drum sounds, an outboard reverb unit to provide maximum ambience, and a noise gate to abruptly silence the track(s). The sound of the signal "recovering" after being severely compressed and reverberated intensifies the effect of the

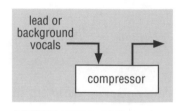

Smooth Vocals

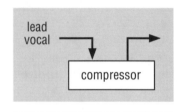

Breathy Vocals

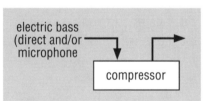

Sustained Bass

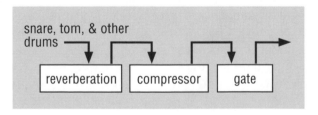

Drums O'Doom

noise gate. The onset of gating should be timed to suit the music.

The reverb unit is the first in the chain (after the source sound, of course) and should be set to a concert hall or plate program with a long decay. Make sure that the reverb's pre-delay is null (0 milliseconds).

The compression ratio should be an over-the-top ∞:1, with a very fast attack time and a threshold level 15 to 40 dB below the peak. You can vary the release time to taste. The noise gate should have an expansion ratio of 1:∞, with a moderately fast release time. Attack and hold times and the threshold level can be set to suit the demands of the music.

Thick and Chunky Guitar. Power chords! Power chords! By applying different amounts of compression to two different mic perspectives, you can make even AC/DC proud. Place microphone A close to the guitar amp speaker and set a compression ratio of 8:1 on compressor A. The high compression mixed with a fast attack time will cause the guitar sound to "pump." The release time also should be moderately fast, and the threshold level

should be 6 dB to 20 dB below the peak.

Use microphone B as a room mic, placing it at least six to ten feet away from the speaker cabinet. You're going for a warm, sustained sound on this mic, so set compressor B's compression ratio at 5:1 with a moderate attack time and a slow release time. The threshold level should be 6 dB to 20 dB below the peak.

Radio Mix. Want to produce a tight, slamming mix for the dance club or radio? Set your compression ratio between 2:1 and 3:1, with a threshold level 2 dB to 4 dB below the peak. Use a moderate attack time and a slow release time.

FAST RELEASE
See, I told you not to be scared—dynamics processing is easy once you understand it! And it not only solves nagging sonic problems, it can produce some pretty hip effects as well. In your informed hands, a dynamics processor now is a powerful and versatile tool. •

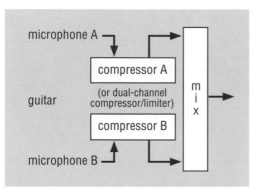

Thick and Chunky Guitar

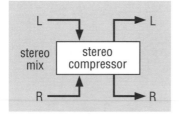

Radio Mix

VCAs and Side-Chains

Central to most dynamics processors is a small circuit known as a *voltage-controlled amplifier* (VCA). Once incoming signals cross the threshold level, the VCA kicks in and begins to attenuate, or reduce, levels. The amount and rate of reduction depends upon the type of processing (compression, expansion, limiting, etc.) and the various control settings.

Normally, the VCA is controlled by whatever signal is at the processor's input. However, many processors allow you to access the VCA's electronic control input via an external *side-chain* (some boxes call it a *detector*, *key*, *control*, or *trigger* input). Once you connect something to the side-chain input, that external source controls how much dynamic processing occurs and when it starts (Fig. 3).

For example, a conventional noise gate application might be silencing an electric bass between performances. In this situation, the gate's VCA is controlled by level changes

in the bass signal. (When the bassist stops playing, the input signal falls below the set threshold, and the gate shuts down the audio.) But if we were to connect the "kick drum" output of a drum machine to the side-chain input, the level of the kick drum would control the VCA. In effect, the kick drum would turn the bass "off and on" with each kick, producing an ultra-tight bass/drum groove.

Keep in mind that side-chain signals only control how the *incoming* audio is pro-

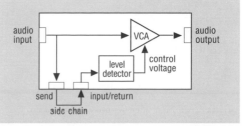

FIG. 3
Block diagram of a generic dynamics processor with a side-chain.

cessed; the side-chain signal is not fed to the processor's outputs. Therefore, unless we simultaneously feed the kick drum signal to the mixer, we won't hear any kick.

4

Marketing
Your Demo

Shopping Your Demo Tape

BE HONEST: How many demo cassettes or master recordings are hiding in your closet? Don't play dumb. Every musician has recorded a demo that seemed destined to win a label or publishing contract. But something happened. Maybe the vocal failed to send shivers down your spine, or the mix didn't sound right, or the song—after countless listens—just didn't seem good enough. In short, you chickened out. The tape was tossed into your secret garden of "lost masterpieces," and no industry ears heard one note.

Well, you'll never get a break if the industry is deaf to your work. You've got to get those demos out of the closet and into someone's hands, or you're just teasing yourself about seeking a career in music. So, for the sake of *your* career, I'm going to be your drill sergeant. I'm going to tell you how to submit a demo and where to send it. All you need are the guts to drop a package into the mail.

TAKING THE HEAT

The reason some musicians cower at the prospect of shopping their work is simple: Submitting demo tapes to industry pros is an excruciating experience. It is not an A&R person's job to deliver polite comments about unsuitable material or nurture your commercially unproven talents. If you don't have what it takes, they're not shy about telling you. (Or worse yet, they may simply ignore you!)

Here's a quick reality check: The entertainment business is a profit industry, and record executives are commissioned to find marketable artists and/or songs that will increase a label's revenues. I'll make things a little clearer: The music industry is not run by artists for the sole purpose of enriching society; rather, it is directed by corporate business interests who crave profit margins wider than the Grand Canyon.

Locked in mortal combat with the balance sheet, an A&R executive's job security often is measured in minutes. Signing one artist that doesn't meet sales projections can mean the "former" executive ends up working at K-Mart before the next *Billboard* hits the newsstands. This situation explains why many A&R people should be excused for not empathizing with your artistic pain and suffering. Give them hits and (maybe) they'll give you a shoulder to cry on.

Few musicians understand that pursuing a commercial music career opens the deepest chambers of your soul to the often-witless criticism of The Public. The bottom line is, if you can't take a punch, you're excused from reading the rest of this chapter.

by Michael Molenda

DOING THE DEED

Okay, you've survived the horror stories. Now let's get to work. There is a definite procedure for submitting demo tapes to industry professionals. Even though this procedure is documented in just about every music-business publication, it has remained a dark secret shared only by an increasingly small band of artists. This must be the reason my production company receives countless unsolicited tapes and handwritten inquiries scrawled (in pencil) on binder paper.

Hey, wake up! No one gets points for messing with professional etiquette. When I receive sloppy submission letters I can assume only two things: The artist cares so little about his or her work that they can't manage a proper submission query, or the artist disrespects my position in the industry *and* the value of my time. I know many other industry pros feel the same

ALBERTO TOLOT

way. Believe me, no one enjoys deciphering epic ramblings from artists who "guarantee" that their tape is chock full of hits. So, to save present (and future) A&R executives from dealing with the bitter fruits of ignorance, here is the "secret" submission procedure.

Ask permission. Never send a tape without first getting approval. Even if a publisher or record label claims to accept unsolicited material, be courteous and forward a query letter before you send off your tape. Query letters should be

typewritten and should include the contact person's full name. ("To whom it may concern" is not an appropriate greeting; do some research and find out who auditions tapes for the company.) Do not put your creative history in the text of the letter. Simply state that you are seeking permission to submit a demo tape consisting of, for example, three songs. Be sure to include a self-addressed (and stamped) reply postcard.

Send a clear message. If you receive permission to submit your work, compile a well-documented package. First, type a brief cover letter thanking the contact person for his or her interest. Be concise. If a biography is requested, make it short (one or two paragraphs is ideal) and include a black and white, 8 x 10 glossy photo. Be sure that your name, address, and telephone number are marked on the cassette cover and on the cassette itself. Don't forget to include a stamped, self-addressed envelope big enough to facilitate return of all your materials.

Follow up. Two weeks after you mail the package, call the contact person to confirm receipt of your materials. Do not badger them or seek a personal critique over the telephone. If they haven't received your package, politely inform them that you'll check again in another week. Also, you should always be sure that your package made it into the right hands.

Be patient. Once you've confirmed the contact person has your tape, relax a bit. Don't become an annoyance by invoking "the squeaky wheel gets the grease" theorem; many industry people will just toss your tape into the Never-Never Land pile. However, if you don't hear anything within a month, call to inquire about your status. Do not sound anxious or pushy. You'll find that many executives actually apologize for delays and may even offer a timeline for getting back to you.

Be gracious. If an industry pro rejects your tape, type them a short letter thanking them for their time and consideration. Professionals appreciate such common courtesy—even if they don't reply—and may remember your name fondly when you ask to submit your next demo. (You

You're gonna love this one. In 1986, a duo called Times Two made a demo tape of electronic pop and shopped for a record deal during a two-week vacation in Los Angeles. They signed with Reprise Records before the vacation ended (and actually charted two minor hits in the late 1980s). You can rationalize all you want that stuff like this never happens. It happens.

weren't thinking of giving up after one try, were you?)

PATHS OF GLORY

Now that you've got the submission procedure, you'll need some places to submit. Some of these ideas are obvious, but I've included a few practical insights for each venue. And don't hope for a home run on your premiere submission.

"Submitting a demo is usually the beginning of an artist's dialog with the industry," says record promoter and label publicist Nadine Condon. "If an A&R rep thinks you have talent, they'll *ask* you to stay in touch, hoping that down the line you'll come up with something they can work with."

Record labels. A direct submission to a record company puts the chances of scoring a deal into the same statistical stratosphere as breaking the bank at Monte Carlo. But people *do* get signed, so why not you? However, be smart. Don't "shotgun submit" to every label in the world. Such lunacy only wastes time and money. Do some market research and determine which labels routinely exploit your style of music. Once you've narrowed the market focus, religiously follow all rules of submission. Remember that in seeking notice from overworked A&R departments—who must swim through thousands of unsolicited tapes from whiny, untalented dream-weavers—one misstep equals doom.

Music publishers. Publishing companies are often-overlooked pathways to a record deal, so don't consider publishers as solely "tune traders." Many publishers sign up promising artists and producers—as long as they can write their own material—and help them seek record contracts. The payback is obvious: A full album of artist-penned tunes can generate sizable revenue because the publisher is entitled to publishing royalties based on sales and airplay. To distinguish yourself from the legions of non-performing songwriters seeking staff-writing or single-song deals, be sure to include the appropriate "slashes" in your submission letter (i.e., producer/songwriter, artist/songwriter, artist/producer/songwriter, etc.).

Management firms. Good managers constantly look toward the future. A firm may represent today's hottest acts, but today's superstars often turn into tomorrow's has-beens. Ambitious artists can win a manager's support by nurturing a casual relationship based on increasingly commercial demo tapes.

Entertainment lawyers. Some music attorneys aspire to be artist managers, record company executives, and even producers. Of course, pulling off such a career change requires a marketable "flagship" artist. Get the picture? But even if a music lawyer doesn't become directly involved in your career, he or she can refer you to valuable industry contacts. It pays to keep reputable attorneys updated on your career, but beware of less-dignified lawyers who charge fees to listen to demos. If they're seriously looking for acts to shop or develop, they should listen to your demo for free.

Performance rights societies. BMI, ASCAP, and SESAC offer many services to aspiring songwriters and recording art-

Pete Townshend (arguably rock music's preeminent demo tape artist) produced hundreds of tracks in his well-equipped home studios. Those who heard his demo tapes of material for The Who often stated that Townshend's versions were far better than the band releases.

ists. BMI, for example, offers frequent new-music concerts that showcase unsigned artists to the industry. In addition, each society has executives who routinely monitor up-and-coming artists. Make sure these people have your latest demo. A&R executives often seek counsel from these societies, so it pays to be the next name on their lips when the labels call.

Songwriter associations. Songwriter associations can be life buoys for frustrated composers. If you're having difficulty getting industry pros to listen to your material, most songwriter associations sponsor events—often called "demo derbies" or "cassette roulette"—where members can play their demos face-to-face with A&R executives or publishers. In addition, many associations also sponsor open-mic performances and songwriter conferences. Non-members usually can check out events by paying a nominal fee.

"We provide a valuable networking conduit for songwriters and the industry," says Ian Crombie, executive director of the Northern California Songwriter's Association. "When you're not in a music capitol such as L.A. or Nashville, it's important that songwriters share resources. And even though our members are competitive, there's a sense of community. For instance, if one of us hears about a good opportunity, it gets around."

THE LONG AND WINDING ROAD
The grand battle cry of hungry musicians is the fact that every successful artist was trashed by someone; quite a few record companies passed on the Beatles before EMI took a chance. However, it can take months or even years between submitting your first demo and signing your first contract. Perseverance is critical: Keep writing, keep improving, keep submit-

ting. If you give up, you're finished. And Sergeant Molenda won't let you give up. So take those demos out of the closet and submit! I'll be watching.   •

Vocalist Steven Tyler and guitarist Joe Perry of Aerosmith don't need to shop their demo tapes; they already sell millions of records. However, even a pro's demo tapes can pay off. Some of the demo tracks recorded in Perry's home studio were so good that they ended up on the album *Get A Grip* (Geffen Records).

Stalking the Deal-Makers

A MODEST PROPOSAL to all musicians seeking a major recording contract: Throw your demo tape in the garbage. This simple action saves time, worry, and postage, and ensures a success ratio equal to sending your tape to every record company in the world. Repeat after me: "An unsolicited demo is landfill."

But seriously, without the aid of someone who can personally address the ears of a record executive, you're just another of thousands of "wannabes" who flood record-company mail rooms with demo tapes. Although occasional exceptions provide manna for the hopeful, the harsh reality of the music business is that someone with industry credibility must present your work to the record labels.

That someone most often is a lawyer.

THE CLOUT FACTOR

"Clout" is a funny word with serious ramifications. Those who have it gain *entree* to the citadels of power. Few aspiring artists wield enough clout to deal with the key business executives who proffer record contracts. That's why the majority of musicians are rewarded for their creative sweat with reams of record-company rejection letters. Although anyone with clout (established managers, producers, agents, etc.) can broker a record deal, entertainment lawyers, by virtue of their immersion in the contractual aspects of the industry, often are the most successful deal-makers.

"A good lawyer is as important as your drummer," says Michael A. Aczon, an entertainment attorney who has worked with Tony! Toni! Toné!, Paris, and producer Al Eaton. "It's part of a lawyer's practice to keep informed on how the music business runs. They work with a lot of record labels, have a broad spectrum of industry contacts, and have a back catalog of deals that comprise a business resume. They also are aware of people moving up the 'food chain' to assume more powerful roles."

In short, an artist can send a thousand tapes to a label and never get past a secretary, while one well-connected lawyer can walk a tape directly into the head office.

There's a reason for this hierarchy. For the most part, the current business orientation of the recording industry has produced administrative, rather than creative, label executives who prefer that "outside" people search for marketable artists. This makes the industry dependent on independent producers, managers, and attorneys to seek out and develop acts.

by Michael Molenda

"There's a tendency for a record company not to trust its own ears," submits attorney Barry Simons, who has negotiated successful deals for Psychefunkapus (Atlantic), Green Things (MCA), the Meat Puppets (London), and Zulu Spear (Capitol). "I call it the Anal-Retentive Record Company Syndrome: They don't know what they want until somebody else wants it."

THE BUZZ BIZ

Enticing a label to "know what it wants" often requires getting other music professionals excited about an artist. This is where a lawyer's industry knowledge and access is a major asset. A good music lawyer looks for key people to start a chain reaction of support for an artist. As Simons puts it, "Creating an industry buzz is an extremely important factor in securing a deal."

One method is to show an artist's work to executives of performing rights societies, such as BMI or ASCAP. These organizations administer song royalties and work closely with publishing companies and record labels. If an artist generates some excitement, a BMI or ASCAP executive may be motivated to bring the act to the attention of record labels and publishing companies.

The Sextants, a San Francisco pop-rock band with Southwestern roots, initially gained momentum through BMI's enthusiam over their songs. BMI's support prompted several publishing companies to make offers. The interest of the publishers—who seek and generate the songs that keep the industry alive—attracted the attention of the labels, and the group was signed to Imago Records in July 1991. (Sadly, the Sextants released one commercially unsuccessful album and were dropped from the label in 1993.)

Collaborating with someone on a label's in-house legal staff is another way to push a tape through the proper channels. It also pays to seek out an attorney who is using a legal practice as a stepping stone to a label's executive suite. Arista Records president Clive Davis is an example of a one-time corporate lawyer ascending to a top creative position. He earned his status by making Columbia Records a rock powerhouse during the 1970s, guiding (among others) the signings of Janis Joplin, Chicago, Santana, and Blood, Sweat, and Tears.

PAYING THE COST

Chasing a record deal isn't cheap. There is no "standard" fee when a lawyer or other agent shops an artist to a record label. Shopping deals have innumerable variations, and often whatever the artist will give up marks the parameters. Lawyers charge by the hour, and the clock is running any time the lawyer works on the artist's behalf. Experienced entertainment attorneys charge between $150 to $300 per hour. While being "on the clock" is an expensive proposition, retaining a lawyer at an hourly rate to shop your work can be cheaper than giving up percentages of your recording deal (i.e., future revenue).

Normally, if a lawyer enters into a shopping deal with an artist, the hourly rate is dismissed in favor of a percentage of the record deal. That percentage can apply to anything from the artist's advance (minus the recording budget) to *all* the artist's record and publishing (song royalty) revenue for the length of the deal.

"It's of paramount importance the artist understand the deal on which the percentage is based," instructs Aczon. "Although

A Whimsical Tale of Woe

The following story is true. Don't waste your time trying to discover who I'm talking about. (I've left the details as vague as possible.) Just don't let this happen to you.

Band X wanted a record deal. They didn't care about the details; they just wanted to be recording artists. Lawyer F found them a manager (another client) and used his contacts in a successful music law firm to secure a deal with a major record label. In compensation, Lawyer F received a hefty percentage of the $250,000 advanced to the band to cover recording costs and other business expenses. (Their new manager also collected a percentage.)

Because Lawyer F was motivated to strike a quick deal, the terms of the contract favored the record company. The band was left little power in determining their career.

The label insisted Band X hire a popular hitmaker to produce their debut album. Producer R cost the band $50,000 in cash, a percentage of gross record sales, and a trip to Europe to record in the producer's studio. (Studio time and room and board were charged to the band.)

When the master was completed, the label decided the tracks weren't "hot" enough and hired (with the band's funds) a megastar's head engineer to remix the album. This exercise cost the band $15,000 cash, first-class airfare (from the megastar's Midwest studio complex), room and board in a 5-star hotel, and a percentage of gross record sales.

When the album finally was released, the band ended up with a pitifully small percentage of its own record profits. The advance fund was decimated to the extent that when the band toured with a major headliner, they couldn't pay their sound technician. The label's (lack of) support was disheartening; the band rarely found their records in the stores. Before the tour ended, the record was dead.

A follow-up album was recorded but never released, and the band's contract was cancelled. Except for one member who plays weddings and local club dates, all of the band members are currently out of the music business.

in a perfect world, it's the lawyer's duty to advise the artist on a deal's ramifications, it's up to the client to understand what is being given away."

ETHICS

Many artists are so desperate for success that they'll sign anything put in front of them (see sidebar, "A Whimsical Tale of Woe"). This is unfortunate, as a bad recording deal can haunt an artist long after the records are in the bargain bins.

"There's a long line of people waiting to eat you up, if you have talent," warns Aczon.

Usually, one of the first people in line at the table is the person shopping your tape. It's a lawyer's duty to point out the pitfalls of a record deal. Since many attorneys use their profession to move into the creative side of the industry, be alert when the lawyer shopping your tape expresses a desire to guide your career. As the lawyer now has a personal stake in your deal, he or she owes it to you to inform you of possible conflicts. Beware of lawyers shopping multiple acts (you may become part of a package deal) and lawyers representing both you and your shopping agent (your interests may get compromised in a dispute). And remember, unless your lawyer also is your manager, he or she probably will disappear once the deal is finalized, but the deal will live on.

Huge legal firms often enjoy privileged status with record labels due to their success and power. Some artists seek the support of these firms, hoping that their lawyers possess the clout to ensure a deal. But keep in mind that if a firm is *really* powerful, the labels probably are big clients. Be extremely skeptical if a firm that does legal work for the labels also claims to be acting in your best interest.

Many lawyers charge a fee for evaluating tapes; this practice is the source of considerable controversy. Artists maintain that if a lawyer is seeking acts to represent, the "audition" process should be free. However, lawyers are not label representatives, and are not paid to sort through boxes of demo tapes. Use your judgment to determine if a lawyer is overcharging for such

consultations. (I maintain, however, that any lawyer seeking acts to shop should not charge the artists for auditioning their demo tapes.)

ARTIST AWARENESS

Seeking a lawyer (or other agent) to shop your tape is a facet of your career development that should not be taken lightly or clouded by hubris. Bad deals destroy careers. It's the responsibility of an artist to determine if they are ready to be seriously shopped. This means more than writing songs, rehearsing a band, and having the right haircut.

"A lot of artists have a very narrow idea of what it takes to get signed," notes Simons. "Often, they think one killer demo equals a deal. That's hardly ever the case. The label people will certainly want to see the band perform live and then audition more material before making a decision."

The first step is knowing what type of deal you want the lawyer to negotiate (see sidebar, "A Basic Deal Menu"). Most artists

A Basic Deal Menu

MAJOR-LABEL RECORDING CONTRACT. This is the jackpot of all jackpots, *if* the label promotes your act. In a perfect world, the company advances you the funds to set up a business entity, buy equipment, record an album, and (if you're lucky) shoot a video and/or tour.

INDEPENDENT-LABEL RECORDING CONTRACT. These typically are special-interest labels set up by people who actually like music for the sake of music. Deals often are "co-op": The artist pays all recording costs and the label underwrites pressing and distribution. Some labels offer small recording budgets.

PUBLISHING CONTRACT. These deals are made solely for an artist's compositions (songs). Since it's in a publisher's best interest to have a client's work commercially exploited, they may assist an artist in securing a major recording contract. Publishing revenue can supply an artist with enough financial freedom to work full-time developing a recording act.

PRODUCTION CONTRACT. A substantial percentage of major-label deals are made through independent producers who sign an artist, develop and record them, and furnish the artist's services to a record company. This is called an "all-in" deal, because the label gets an artist and producer. Sometimes the producer supplies a label with a finished master.

DEVELOPMENT DEAL. Sometimes a label gives a promising artist a small budget with which to record demos. Basically, the label is buying "future options" for an artist who is not quite ready for a big record contract. While the artist's services are locked down for a set time, the label can evaluate his or her creative growth and suitability for commercial exploitation.
—*Michael Molenda and Michael A. Aczon*

are notoriously naive about where they fit on the career development chart.

Business affairs must be put in order so the lawyer has an uncontested right to represent the artist's interests. The lawyer must know every aspect of an artist's contractual obligations to determine whether previous deals could impair label negotiations. It's surprising how often an artist doesn't own the master tape being shopped. Sometimes a recording studio or other outside investor offers free studio time to an artist in exchange for recouped costs and a percentage of the deal, should the artist sign a major-label contract. In these instances, the studio (or investor) may own the master tape.

Other possible problems involve management and production contracts. The lawyer's ability to negotiate in the artist's behalf is severely limited if the major player in a deal is the manager or producer. An artist must know the difference between *employing* a producer and *being employed by* a producer.

As you can see, it's often a good idea to involve a lawyer or informed legal consultant in your career before you start shopping labels. The bargaining table is not a good place for the past to rear its ugly head.

DECISIONS, DECISIONS

It's important that you make an informed choice regarding who shops your tape, since this person is acting in your behalf.

He or she is your guide through some rocky terrain. An office with gold records shimmering from every wall is a monument to past success, not insurance that your project will join the trophy case. Some lawyers will understand your music, others won't. It's to an artist's advantage to find a lawyer who is sensitive to their individual voice.

"Anyone who shops your music should like it," Aczon insists. "They're going to be playing your tape over and over to many different people. A certain level of enthusiasm is important. If the [shopping] agent isn't excited about the act, the deal is over before it starts."

Artists also should decide if they really want to join the music *business.* The machinations of contract dealings take the romance out of making music. Seeking a recording deal often prompts a devastating career analysis. This is the real stuff. It has nothing to do with your first rush at hearing the Beatles, or the tingles that run up your spine when you hold a guitar. It's about selling records, which is only slightly cooler than selling laundry detergent, and many talented musicians are forever broken by the experience.

"It is never easy to get a record deal," declares Simons. "And it's not an enviable job to represent artists you believe in to record executives who are basically clowns. There are so few people I respect in this industry, I can barely remember who they are." •

Pressing It Yourself

HAVING AN ALBUM can do a lot of things for an artist. First of all, it allows more people to experience your musical talents. Second, it provides a tangible way of making money, via off-stage gig sales, mail order, and retail outlets (such as book and record stores). But most important of all, your record propels you into the elite stratosphere of recording artists, opening new avenues of publicity through radio airplay and record reviews. Another significant aspect (although less tangible) is the "cool" factor: An album is far more impressive than a demo tape when you're dealing with the business realities of negotiating with clubs, and getting *good* gigs.

Simply put, an album can be a very good tool for the serious musical artist. It's even better when it says "Warner Bros." somewhere on the outside of the package, but until the major record labels call, doing it yourself is the next best thing.

FINANCIAL CONSIDERATIONS

One of the toughest decisions to make is deciding what percentage of your release is cassette or CD. The vinyl record is pretty much dead these days, although the classic 7-inch, 45 rpm vinyl single is making a comeback with alternative and punk music consumers. But if the purpose of your release is in-store sales and airplay, CDs are a must. For off-stage sales, a 50/50 mix of CDs and cassettes seems to be the norm. If you decide to go CD-only, you'll be amazed at the number of potential customers who *don't* have CD players. Of course, a major advantage of cassettes is the ability to do short runs of 25, 50, or 100, so your initial investment can be a lot lower.

By their very nature, CDs are better suited to larger production runs, typically 500 and up. Some CD plants have minimum orders of 1,000-2,000 units, while others will begrudgingly press smaller orders. (Unfortunately, many manufacturers charge a per-disc rate so high that the 500-disc order often costs the same as 1,000 discs.)

A similar situation exists with printing CD booklets and cassette insert cards. With small orders, a majority of the printing costs include the labor for pre-press preparation, printing plates, etc. Therefore, you might find it advantageous to print, say, 2,000 pieces (even though your release is only 1,000 units), and *by George Petersen* save the additional 1,000 in case you need to reorder. On a recent project I produced, the cost of printing 1,000 four-color CD books was $695; the price for 2,000 books was $795. Therefore, the per-unit cost of the first 1,000 was nearly 70 cents, while the additional 1,000 were a dime apiece. Sometimes it pays to think ahead.

Another tough question is deciding how many units you need. An order for 1,000 is a *lot* of albums to move, unless you're gigging a lot and have plenty of retail outlets available. It ain't cheap either: We're talking about a major outlay of cash. But if you're in a band (as opposed to a solo artist), you have a number of financial sources to tap into.

One solution that I have long recommended is the following: Let each person in the band contribute an equal share of the costs. When the product arrives, each band member gets some of the albums, with the remainder used for sales and promotion. For example, from an order of 1,000, each member of a five-piece group could get 100 albums to give to their friends (all of whom want free copies, of course), with 500 units for in-store and off-stage sales and radio/press promos.

PLANNING FOR SUCCESS

No matter how you record your tracks, the time to start thinking about the album is *before* you mix.

If you're mixing to analog tape, use the highest tape speed available; 15 ips is probably the best compromise, because 7.5 ips suffers from reduced audio quality, while 30 ips requires high-end machines. (Because of this, many small tape duplication companies can't work with 30 ips master tapes.) Whenever doing any analog recording, Dolby Spectral Recording noise reduction (not to be confused with Dolby A, B, C, or S) is a real godsend, offering audio specs that can surpass digital, while providing all the editing simplicity of analog tape. If you're mixing at a home studio (or at a pro facility that doesn't have SR) you might look into the possibility of renting a 2-channel SR unit for your mix.

If you mix to DAT, things get a bit more complicated. Record at a sampling rate of 44.1 kHz, with pre-emphasis switched off. (If there's no emphasis switch on the deck, then don't worry it.) Make sure that record levels *never* exceed 0 dB: Digital overload is something no one wants to hear, and it's a flaw that is virtually impossible to correct at a later date.

Calibration/alignment tones are essential at the head of your mix tapes: DAT should have one minute of 1kHz recorded on both channels at 0 dB. Analog tapes should have one minute each of 1 kHz, 100 Hz, and 10 kHz, recorded on both channels at your maximum reference level, along with tones for Dolby A or SR (if applicable).

Before you start editing your tapes, you should work out the order of cuts on the album. I usually do this by making several cassette copies of the final mixes, trying out tracks in different orders, and paying attention to the pacing of the cuts. I even check out how the musical keys of songs blend together when they're played back to back. You can save a lot of (expensive) studio time by having a list of the tracks you want, along with their playing times, *before* you start the editing process.

In this pre-editing phase, there are a couple of things to consider. On a cassette tape release, the final product comes out nicer when both sides are approximately the same length. On a CD release, there's no need to worry about the two sides, but you should try to keep the total running time less than 70 minutes and the total number of tunes under 20. In some cases, it may be possible to exceed these limits— I have heard of CDs going as long as 85 minutes, and 99 tracks are common on sound effects discs—but such exceptions usually are expensive and are only granted by special dispensation at the whim of the CD plant.

EDITING

Way back when, in the dinosaur days of vinyl records, it was common practice to put about six seconds of silence between tracks. The reason for this was to provide a visual "band" on the disc, to allow for easy cueing. However, in these days of cassettes and CDs, such a requirement does not exist. So feel free to edit the tunes any way you like.

Analog editing usually is nothing more than sequencing the cuts in the order you desire by splicing the songs and placing white leader tape between cuts. An entire album often can be edited in one hour. No sweat. Just make sure that you put tones on the head, and if the edit is done for cassette release, leave plenty of leader between the sides. (You also could put each side on a separate reel of tape.)

Digital editing gets a bit more tricky; it's impossible to physically splice a DAT cassette. Fortunately, there are a couple of alternatives. The simplest method of editing a digital tape is to transfer it to a reel-to-reel digital (Mitsubishi, Sony, or Studer) or analog (15 or 30 ips with Dolby SR) format and physically splice the tunes in the order desired. Corrective equalization and/or minor level changes can be made during the transfer, and the edited version then can be copied over to a Sony PCM-1630 or PCM-1610 recorder (the required format for a compact disc master tape; the system uses ³/₄-inch U-matic video tape to store the digitized information), or to a DAT recorder to create a copy that can be sent to the cassette duplicator.

However, a relatively cost-effective way to keep DAT editing in the digital domain is to transfer the tracks into a disk-based digital recording/editing workstation. While these computer-based systems tend not to be overly expensive (from a pro audio standpoint), they require massive amounts of hard-disk storage, which can add up quickly to a huge chunk of change. Over 600 MB of disk space is required to handle a CD editing project, with 720 MB (or more) preferred for longer projects.

While editing within the workstation environment is relatively fast, it does require a fair amount of patience, particularly since the tunes must be loaded into the system in real time. Ditto for off-loading the final edited version (to DAT or PCM-1630). But once you're in the workstation, all kinds of creative options are available, such as programmable crossfades between songs, extending (or shortening) a song by duplicating (or deleting) a chorus or verse and copying it elsewhere in the tune, or instantly hearing different versions of the same edit (without destroying the original). Some systems also offer digital equalization and level control.

At this point, it's a good idea to make a safety copy (usually on DAT) of the edited album. Keep the safety in a secure place, just in case disaster strikes. It's a well-known fact that throughout the entire history of recorded audio, no master tape has ever been lost or damaged when a digital safety copy was readily available.

Before you leave that mastering or pre-mastering facility, you'll need to create a "PQ" log sheet to accompany your PCM-1630 master tape to the CD plant (**Fig. 1**). The sheet really is nothing more than a list

Fantasy Mastering			
Client/Label: Sound & Vision Records			
Catalog #: SV2507			
Artist/Program: ASCOT JACKET			
MASTER TAPE TIMING SHEET	**Description:** "The Infamous Ascot Jacket"		
Pg 1 of 1 Date 8-17-93 By MM	**Format:** PCM-1630, (44.1) (No Emph), SMPTE on Aux 2		
	Remarks: —		

TRACK No.	TITLE	REMARKS/NOISES	TIME CODE hr + min + sec + fr.
1	Symphony of Life	✓	00.02.00.00 / 00.05.59.04
2	Fool's Parade	✓	00.06.01.17 / 00.08.55.23
3	The King Must Die	✓	00.08.58.07 / 00.12.55.16
4	Why Do You Want Me?	Crossfade	00.12.55.17 / 00.17.30.00
5	Lines in the Dark	✓	00.17.32.27 / 00.23.26.20
6	She's Got Things (No One Talks About)	✓	00.23.29.17 / 00.29.36.20
7	I've Waited So Long	✓	00.29.36.21 / 00.34.02.17
8	Upside Down	✓	00.34.04.20 / 00.37.00.00
9	Undertow	✓	00.37.04.01 / 00.40.07.20
10	Where Did All The Love Go?	✓	00.40.10.05 / 00.42.55.15

of all the song titles, with their start and stop times referenced to a SMPTE time code track (30 frames per second, non-drop-frame rate), along with the location and type of calibration tones on the tape. The "PQ" part of the name comes from the P-Q sector in the CD format's subcode that includes all track indexing and timing data.

Generally, most CD plants require all PCM-1630 master tapes to have two

FIG. 1

A PQ sheet for a CD master tape includes information on the order and length of each song, whether crossfades were used, the lengths of between-song silences, and other important mastering data.

minutes of digital silence before *and* after the music program. The PQ sheet also carries information as to whether any songs are cross-faded, the exact length of silence between cuts, and frame-accurate running times for songs. When your tape arrives at the CD plant, a technician enters the cue points from your PQ log into a PQ editor that transfers your cue points into the subcode area of the CD master.

PRESSING AND PACKAGING

Now the real fun begins. Armed with your edited analog or digital master tape, you're ready to start hunting for a duplicator or replicator that suits your needs and budget. Duplicators and pressing plants come in every conceivable variety: large or small, "do-it-all" or specialty shops. The trick is to find the supplier that best suits your project. While there are less than 20 CD duplicators in North America—and they don't want to be bothered with small orders—there are dozens of companies that act as brokers and can handle every step of your CD project, including editing, artwork, pressing, packaging, and even drop-shipping to customers and retailers.

If you decide to take the *a la carte* route—contracting with separate printing and pressing companies—keep in mind that most tape duplicators and CD sources will insert customer-supplied printed materials into the finished product. However, the size tolerances of the automatic packaging equipment can be extremely exacting, often ±0.5 mm or tighter. So before you leap, check with your duplicator regarding size specifications, and make sure the printer you select has experience doing CD or cassette inserts.

Your project's graphic design can be as simple or complex as you want (or can afford). Unless you're adept at graphics, you might want to leave this phase to a professional. Some CD/tape brokers offer complete design packages, including typesetting all the materials and incorporating your band's logo and/or photo into the finished product. Based on the samples of efforts I've seen, the results run the gamut from serviceable to spectacular. If in doubt, ask to see some of their samples before you proceed.

MICHAEL DWORNIK

Regarding graphics, there are a couple of things that always seem to be overlooked: the cassette tape label (for *both* sides of the tape) and the label on the CD itself. Besides the usual info, the CD label must also have an official "Compact Disc Digital Audio" logo; the cassette label should display the type of tape used (especially if it's CrO_2) and the type of noise reduction (such as Dolby B or C), if applicable.

STICKING WITH TAPE

Myriad possibilities exist when choosing a tape duplicator. Real-time duplicators offer potentially higher audio quality, but usually charge significantly more than high-speed duplication systems. Generally, if your order is less than 200 tapes, you're better off going with a real-time duplicator. From 200 to 500 tapes, it's generally a coin-toss affair, and with orders more than 500 units, high speed is generally the way to go. However, as with anything else in life, there are exceptions: I've heard some high-speed duplication that rivaled the best real-time systems.

Two major variables to contend with are the tape stock used for duplication and the shell (cassette housing) itself. A cheap shell often can make the finest tape stock sound like garbage, and the finest shell will do little to improve the sound of a low-quality tape formulation. Bite the bullet and insist on the best tape and shells available for your project. Believe me, there's a major, audible difference, and

Smart bands don't wait for the blessing of the major labels to sell records. In 1983, the Hooters released a self-produced cassette album that sold 100,000 copies regionally. When the band *did* get a major record deal, they delivered the monster hit "All You Zombies" and became—for a brief period in the mid-1980s— the darlings of MTV.

the music is the most important thing, right? Before choosing a duplicator, ask for samples of projects recorded on the various tape/shell grades, then listen and decide for yourself.

There are a couple of other aesthetic points to consider: the selection of shell colors (black, white, and clear are most popular) and ink colors for the cassette label. If your project involves more than 300 cassettes, most duplicators can print the label information directly on the shell; with lower runs, this info usually is printed on adhesive labels (also available in many colors) that are applied to the cassette.

SOME FINAL CONSIDERATIONS

Before getting too wrapped up in all this, take a moment to sit back and sort a few things out. The first thing you need to do is put together a budget, which would include editing and/or mastering time and supplies, design and typesetting charges (plus materials), photo shoots and prints, printing charges, CD or tape replication, jewel boxes and cassette cases, packaging; shipping, sales tax (if applicable), the original recording/mixing costs, phone calls, and just about anything else you can think of. Now add to that a 10-20% contingency fee (for those unexpected emergencies), and you should be right on the mark.

Also keep in mind that most tape, CD, and printing plants have a clause in their contracts stating that all orders are subject to a ±10 percent over/under run. This means that your 1,000 unit order could theoretically range anywhere from 900 to 1,100 pieces. The norm usually is in the ± 5 percent range, and you will be billed for the actual quantity shipped. In the worst-case scenario (assuming a separate printer and CD plant), you could wind up paying for 1,100 CDs and have only 900 booklets!

Now, look at your timetable. How long do you expect this process to take? Will any of your suppliers deliver late? (Graphics always seem to take forever.) What is the promised turnaround time for the CD/ tape plant? (Did you know that late July through October is the busiest time of the year, as these companies gear up to deliver product to be on store shelves before the holidays?) How much shipping time is required? I've heard of countless bands that scheduled record-release parties and the only "no-shows" were the records. Don't let this happen to you.

And don't forget about insurance. If you have to mail your master tape and artwork, spend the extra cash and send it by an overnight service, insured. Another type of "insurance" is to make sure that *everything* you send out has your name,

ANDI BULL

address, and phone number on it. This is especially true for your log sheets, graphics, and master tapes, which should all be marked inside the tape box, on the outside, and on the tape itself. Don't forget to make a safety copy of the master before it gets mailed off to some distant locale.

When your final product comes back, don't forget to protect your work by copyrighting the sound recording with Copyright Form SR. Forms are available through the Copyright Office in Washington, DC. A nominal filing fee and two copies of the finished work are required to secure a copyright.

Admittedly, struggling through all this information can be tedious. But if you're planning to release your own album, forewarned is forearmed. Ready for the next big step in your career? Just take your time and do it right.   •

The classic 45 rpm vinyl single ain't dead yet. It has become the media of choice in alternative music circles, allowing unsigned bands an inexpensive vehicle for self-promotion. San Francisco's Screaming Bloody Marys consistently release "7-inchers"—on red vinyl, no less—and have earned small pockets of fans all over the world.

The Secret World of Record Promotion

ONE OF THE MOST MISUNDERSTOOD ASPECTS OF THE MUSIC BUSINESS is record promotion; a mysterious aura always has surrounded promoters. If you believe the muckrakers, independent promoters are nothing more than criminals who trade money and drugs for radio airplay. But while the music business *does* have its share of borderline characters, the majority of record promoters are far from purveyors of payola.

Basically, record promoters are hard-working people immersed in the responsibility of getting an artist's work out to the public. *How* they work is up to the individual, but *what* they do is simple: They get records played on the radio.

RADIO, RADIO

Radio stations are divided into different stylistic formats. The current major categories are contemporary hit radio (CHR), album-oriented radio (AOR), urban, country, adult contemporary (AC), alternative/college, metal, jazz, rap, and new age/adult alternative. Each week, trade publications track the stations in every category and compile information for the powerful and influential charts that list the records receiving the most national airplay.

These charts are vital to a record's success, because radio stations are blatant copycats. When a station sees a record is "hot" on similarly formatted stations, it often adds the record to its playlist. Then, as more stations add the record, its chart position rises, and the hoped-for journey to the top of the charts begins.

Traditionally, the charts also help record labels determine marketing strategies for a particular release. The amount of money a label spends on advertising, sales, and promotion for a record often is directly related to how high the record charts. Records that don't generate chart action usually are ignored by the major labels and often die a dismal death in record-shop bargain bins.

PROMOTING SUCCESS

Unfortunately, shaking some action on the charts is not an easy gig. Because of the overwhelming number of current releases, merely sending a record to a radio station won't get it played, even if you're Sony Music. Station program directors (PDs) and music directors (MDs) usually receive 50 new records a week. The competition for airtime is brutal. Major labels attack the competition with in-house promotion departments whose sole responsibility is to personally deliver records to radio stations. Promotion staffs also place initial introductory calls to the station describing the current release, make follow-up calls informing the station of the release's current success on other stations, wine and dine PDs and

by Nadine Condon

MDs, and develop promotional give-aways and contest trips that enhance the record's appeal to radio personnel and consumers.

However, in-house promotional staffs often are overwhelmed by the sheer number of their label's releases. To effectively work the overflow, labels hire independent record promoters, or *indies*. Indies are specialists who have nurtured close personal and professional relationships with the PDs and MDs of important radio stations. Because the key to good promotion is personal contacts, these people are incredibly valuable. They act as a conduit between a label and a station, and can get through to a PD or MD when others can't. For example, if 50 promotion reps are calling a station, the PD is most likely to return the calls of people he or she knows, likes, and trusts.

The price for an indie's contacts and persuasive talents varies according to his or her industry standing and success record, the format being promoted, and the type of project. Costs range from $400 to $1,000 per week for a specified number of weeks, or a flat fee of $5,000 to $20,000 for the "life of the project" (generally considered to be ten weeks).

● Learning a Hard Lesson

Back in the early 1980s, I released a solo album on Amorous Records, a small San Francisco label run by artist-manager Stephen M.H. Braitman. The deal was typical of most independent-label contracts: I paid my own recording costs, and the label manufactured the record and secured an independent distribution deal.

It was soon apparent that we weren't selling any records by wishing and hoping. A meeting between Braitman and the label's three artists (myself, Times Beach, and House of Pants) produced the bold plan to bankroll an outreach program to college radio and major-market FM stations. The concept of professional record promoters servicing small independent labels was underdeveloped at this time, so the do-it-yourself approach seemed the best way to fight anonymity (and the dire equation of "no airplay and no sales equals a bankrupt label").

Amorous Records installed a "cut rate" long distance carrier on the office phone and paid for national college and major market radio lists. The bands agreed to reimburse Amorous for phone calls in our behalf (a more immediate twist on the "recoupable" promotional budget) and instituted a program of telephone warfare where each band spent a specified amount of time harassing PDs and MDs, logging responses, and mailing records to interested stations.

The initial response was quite impressive. The stations started mailing their playlists to the Amorous office, and within two months my record was being played nationally on more than 55 radio stations. (The eventual final tally was 92 stations, of which 67 were college and 25 were AOR.)

Unfortunately, our naivete and lack of experience started to kill us. We didn't think to recommend a song as a "single," so each station picked a favorite cut. It was interesting to see the diversity of songs played, but the lack of a cut on which to target serious promotional efforts stalled successful marketing. Also, the telephone bills and mailing costs were sinking the bands and the label. No one was sufficiently capitalized to handle monthly costs averaging $300 for phone bills, $125 for postage, and $75 for mailing, printing, and packaging. In addition, our distributor was rather sluggish at moving our records, so actual sales remained slow.

All the time and expense provided the bands tons of ego gratification and enough playlists to wallpaper a kitchen, but the eternal bottom line—revenue—wasn't justifying the operation. Within eight months, the bands and label agreed to abort the promotional push. Without sustained airplay, my record died like a self-fulfilling prophecy. The distributors returned boxes of unsold goods (many of which still reside in my parents' attic—sorry, Mom and Dad), and Amorous Records faded into history as just another seminal—albeit unsuccessful—new wave label.

A few years later, when my band The Wobblies was courted by the (then) West German label Marimba, I had no reservations about agreeing to a substantial recoupable budget for independent promotion. I had learned my lesson. —*Michael Molenda*

Savvy artist managers often negotiate with the labels to hire indies for their clients. This is smart business, as it ensures that the artist won't get lost in the shuffle of releases promoted by the label. The fee for independent promotion is paid by the artist's promotional budget—which may or may not be recoupable by the label—and the label writes the checks.

PROMOTING SMALL LABELS

Smaller independent labels perceive chart action differently than the majors. The life of an independent record is not greatly influenced by chart numbers, as the company may only have a regional emphasis or a cult (niche) market. However, if a small label does chart a record, it greatly increases industry status, credibility, and visibility. Self-released records that chart usually make a big splash at major-label A&R departments.

However, the promotional options facing an independent or self-released record are limited. Frankly speaking, most CHR stations only play major-label releases, so it's a waste of time badgering them. It's better to first get a record happening in a more receptive arena. College, alternative, and other more specialized stations (rap, new age, etc.) usually accept records from smaller independent labels.

Exploiting this specific market are a growing number of small indie promoters who work with small labels and self-released records. Their radio lists are compiled from similarly specialized trade publications such as *College Music Journal* (*CMJ*), *The Gavin Report*, and *Rockpool*. Fees paid to the small indie promoter are more in line with independent label budgets, averaging $200-$250 per week with a four-week minimum. The smaller indies usually commit to calling each station once every two weeks and provide other services, such as promotional mailings.

Obviously, there is no large record label underwriting the promotional costs for self-released or independent projects (unless the label has cut a distribution deal with a major). This means *you* are

paying the bills, so be sure to target your radio audience and hire an indie who specializes in your field. A well-targeted indie is especially important if you're seeking college radio airplay, as there can be a yearly turnover of the students who run the stations. Because of this rapid turnover, it's nearly impossible to form close bonds with PDs and MDs, so the value of a smaller indie lies in his or her knowledge of the station's overall programming. A college station's format usually doesn't change, even if the staff does. However, it's essential that the indie understand the history of what works—and what doesn't work—for a college station's musical format.

A reputable indie promoter should give you a client history that details past successes and a list of stations they service. If you hire them, make sure you receive a detailed breakout every week of your record's activity on each station. This report should include whether the station listened to the record or not, any comments from the PD or MD, and whether the record was tested or added. If the station plays your record, the activity must be reported to the trades and the indie should concentrate on stimulating upward chart movement.

Also, certain professionals within the independent promotion community specialize in niche marketing and other specialized tasks. These include coordinating promotional activities while a band is on tour, contests, and target mailings to special "fan lists."

THE ROAD TO THE CHARTS

The important considerations to remember in record promotion are a band's marketing budget, its short- and long-term career goals, and maintaining professional working relationships with the industry.

Independent promoters are an essential part of a record's equation for success. Any band releasing an independent project should make room in its budget for a promoter. You'll have a tough time getting your music heard without one. •

5

Taking It
From the Pros

Recording Hit Records

WALKING INTO A PROFESSIONAL RE-CORDING STUDIO is like making a pilgrimage to Lourdes: You immerse yourself in its sacred mysteries, and if you're lucky a miracle happens. For the musician, this usually means a hit record. And although the fabric of real miracles is shrouded in divine secrecy, the machinery of hit records is easily defined: You need an artist, instruments, a recording medium, and someone to document the magic. That someone is a recording engineer.

But what do professional recording engineers do that's any different from a knowledgeable home recordist? How do they engage—or disengage—technology to make great-sounding records that seduce the music-loving masses? Well, I've never believed that curiosity killed the cat, so I asked some top engineers who worked on professional projects in a variety of musical styles, from pop to jazz to new age, to talk about the techniques they used to create "hit" records. You'll also learn that technical chops alone can't ensure a sonic masterpiece—the quality of the artist's performance is a vital link in recording great sounds.

Admittedly, not every album profiled here sold a million units, but each certainly qualifies as an important work in its genre. So without further ado, follow me down these dark passages into the citadels of sound.

DRUMS AND BASS
RED HOT CHILI PEPPERS, BLOOD SUGAR SEX MAGIK (WARNER BROTHERS) BRENDAN O'BRIEN, ENGINEER

The band and [producer] Rick Rubin wanted to record the album in a house, so we rented an incredible mansion and brought in a Neve console, an analog 24-track machine, and other necessities. The library became the control room, the grand ballroom was the main studio, an upstairs bedroom was Anthony Kiedis' vocal "booth," and the amps were set up and miked in the basement. All of the basic tracks—drums, bass, and guitar—were recorded live, with the band monitoring their instruments [and Kiedis' vocals] on headphones.

For the song "Give It Away," Chad Smith's drums were placed in this great solarium, which had marble floors and huge glass panes for the walls and ceiling. I used only four mics on the kit: a Shure SM57 on the kick drum, an SM57 on the snare, and two AKG C414s for overheads. Individually, the tracks really didn't sound very good. The kick and snare were thin, and the overheads were pretty washy. But the combination of all the mics sounded amazing.

This arrangement was used pretty much throughout the album. For other songs, I moved the drums back into the

by Michael Molenda

ballroom and miked the toms and hi-hat individually, but I ended up erasing the separate tracks and using only the kick, snare, and overheads. Also, there's hardly any [outboard] reverb used on the record; all the drum reverb you hear is the natural sound of the room. Compression was employed rather sparingly. The overhead mics were run through UREI LA-4s, because the units react slowly and provide a lot of punch without altering the sound too much. I routed the snare microphone through a dbx 160 compressor and left the kick mic alone.

Actually, I recorded everything quite simply. The mic selection wasn't very scientific; if it sounded good, we used it. I used an SM57 on the kick drum because it was the closest mic when I was setting up the kit. The reason the drums sound so kickin' is almost completely due to the fact that Chad is a great drummer.

For the bass tracks, Flea used a Gallien-Krueger amp through a Mesa/Boogie cabinet. At least I'm pretty sure that's what he used—I never saw the rig much because everything was down in the basement! I stuck a large-diaphragm Sony condenser in front of the amp and also took a direct line. Both the miked and direct signals were recorded to separate tracks and compressed to tape with UREI LA-4s. I've found that just about any UREI [compressor] sounds good on basses, because they don't pinch the bottom end.

I know this all sounds pretty anti-technology, and I probably know more than I'd like to admit about [recording] technique. But I believe that the best records have been made by engineers who were also musicians, or who had a lot of musical knowledge. Technique is secondary. On this project in particular, I learned that getting a great performance is the key to producing a great record.

For example, if you're recording a guitar track, and the amp sounds good and the guitarist is playing well, it probably won't matter what microphone you use. Whatever records the performance cleanly onto tape is usually good enough. We even had what we called the "magic mic," a Shure SM57 that sounded great on everything. I'd say 75 percent of the overdubs were tracked with that single micro-

phone. It's kind of funny—the main mic used on this huge multi-platinum record cost about $140.

ELECTRIC GUITARS
CHAGALL GUEVARA, CHAGALL GUEVARA (MCA)
DAVID BRYSON, ENGINEER

Chagall Guevara is a completely guitar-driven band; they all use old Vox AC30 amps with Rickenbacker and Les Paul guitars. Stylistically, it seemed appropriate to go for a simple, straight-up guitar sound. But even so, I'd say that the biggest secret about recording guitars is that there is no secret. Just get a great sound from the guitar and amp, and stick a mic in front of it.

I had the guitar player plug straight in—without any outboard effects—and stand close to his amp. Then I'd position both an Electro-Voice RE20 and a Shure SM57 right near the speaker cone. The RE20 tends to pick up warm tones, while the SM57 delivers brighter timbres. For a room sound, a Neumann U87 was placed about ten feet away from the amp. Tonal selections were based solely on the mic sounds, and often I'd blend all three mics together to get a sound.

The only outside processing was compression, and its use depended on the guitar part. Usually it was employed only to tame dynamics, but compression can also make guitars sound way louder than the actual volume at which they were recorded. Used as an effect, compression can really give you some tough guitar tones.

ACOUSTIC GUITARS
THE RIPPINGTONS, WEEKEND IN MONACO (GRP RECORDS)
RUSS FREEMAN, PRODUCER/ENGINEER

When recording acoustic guitars, I try to use as much of the organic, unprocessed sound as possible. I strive to achieve the sound of the guitar in the room. Basically, I go by the old adage that if you have to over-EQ, you're not miking correctly.

For the song "Where the Road Will Lead Us," I played a classical (nylon-string) guitar and miked it with an AKG C414 angled toward the sound hole and an AKG C452 "dead on" to capture some brightness. The recording environment in my studio is fairly live, as it's a pretty big room, and the floors are all wood. Luckily, my wife can engineer while I'm playing, which saves a lot of running back and forth to check sounds and operate the multitrack deck. The blend of the two microphones was pretty much even.

I used the same miking pattern for the steel-string acoustic on "Moka Java," but I added the direct sound of my Takamine acoustic/electric guitar to the mix. I blended the three inputs together, with most of the sound coming from the C414, added a little of the C452 for brightness, and mixed in the direct sound very subtly, as it tends to pick up a lot of string noise.

I've found that the less compression I use on guitars, the better. When I do compress, I use a UREI tube 1176. I also use very little, if any, equalization and all the tonal processing depends on the needs of the song. The ideal tone usually isn't very difficult to figure out because by the time I record the guitar, the track is almost done. It's painfully obvious where to fit the guitar sonically.

GRAND PIANO
BRUCE STARK, SONG OF HOPE (HEARTS OF SPACE RECORDS) BOB HODAS, ENGINEER

The critical factor in recording a great piano sound—and this should be pretty obvious—is you have to have a good piano in a good room. My favorite saying is, "You can't make chicken salad out of chicken shit." For this record, we rented a marvelous Grotrian Steinweg and brought it to The Site in San Rafael, California.

The Site has a fairly large room with all wood treatment and a huge glass window overlooking a valley. It's pretty live-sounding. We kept the curtains closed on the valley view, partly for acoustics and partly to keep the sun from causing temperature changes that would cause tuning problems. The piano was set up at the far end of the studio, pointing toward the control room, with the lid open full-stick.

I used four mics: three conventional and one stereo. B&K 4011s have a tight pattern, so I stuck them inside the piano. The mic positions were determined by

sticking my head in there to find spots that produced balanced tonalities. A Neumann SM69 stereo tube mic was put in its XY configuration and placed fifteen to twenty feet away from the piano and about eight feet high. A Beyer MC740 was in Omni mode at the far end of the room, about fifteen to eighteen feet in the air. These room mics were moved around until we found spots that sounded the richest.

Song of Hope was recorded direct to DAT, so balancing the mic positions was critical. In the end, the SM69 provided the main piano sound, and the 4011s were mixed in for presence. The 740 was fed into a Quantec XL multi-effect, and only the reverb return was mixed in to provide ambience. Stark's producer, Stephen Hill, loves "space music" and had no qualms about mixing reverb in during the performance and recording the effect to tape.

In addition, we used Meyer CP10 and Massenberg equalizers to shape the piano sound. Nothing radical was done; we merely took out some of the top end and also processed the reverb sends to simulate a larger, softer room. The recording console was a Neve 8058 Class A, and I used Massenberg and EAR tube mic preamps.

I like to go into sessions with the attitude that there is no one way to do something. On this record, we changed things to meet the demands of the song. Bruce didn't even use headphones; he performed as if he were giving a recital. This caused us to have to work out visual cues for certain things, but Bruce's performance was much more relaxed. At the bottom line, it's really the performance that counts. A creative artist, unencumbered by technology and enjoying the touch and sound of a great piano, can deliver an amazing performance.

LEAD VOCALS
WHITNEY HOUSTON, THE BODYGUARD SOUNDTRACK (ARISTA RECORDS) DAVID FRAZER, ENGINEER

With Whitney, you basically push Record, and you've got half the track. If you're not set up, you're in trouble. She is incredibly

fast at getting her performances down and can ad lib very naturally. Her vibrato is like a little flutter— sometimes you don't even realize it's there—and it really energizes a vocal track. She also can double [her vocal performance] very well. She's so precise that when her doubled tracks are mixed together, it sounds like one voice, only fuller.

To record the song "I'm Every Woman," I set up an AKG C414 with a windscreen in a small room at Ocean Way Studios in Los Angeles. Before we started recording, I worked up some basic EQ and compression settings based on the vocal register Whitney was in. I used a Focusrite equalizer as a mic preamp— they sound good and act as a consistent entity from one studio to another—and limited the signal through a Neve stereo compressor.

We have a pretty consistent system of tracking vocals, and this method was employed on "I'm Every Woman." Narada Michael Walden [the track's producer] works singers pretty hard to find the right attitude and phrasing, so we'll typically record ten to twelve vocal tracks for each section of the song: the verse, chorus, and bridge. The final vocal performance is assembled from bits and pieces of these multiple takes. Of course, with Whitney, any one of these takes could be the final track. But Narada always looks for that perfect expression of feeling, which may be more pronounced on one take over another [for a particular section or phrase].

We usually give Whitney two tracks to run down the song before Narada starts critically directing her performance. Much of the final track is often composed of these "run-down" takes, because they're fresh and spontaneous. Narada likes to nail the entire vocal track on the first day. Then he'll check the tracks the next day and decide whether to re-record a few sections.

When Narada approves the final composite vocal track, I'll re-EQ and recompress it slightly to get a blend between the various performances. We'll start from beginning to end to get a good sound, which is sometimes difficult because vocalists sing a little differently from day to day.

To make the combined performances sound natural, we often have to match vocal EQ settings line by line, and sometimes we're changing EQ on syllables. All of this probably sounds pretty crazy, but the real trick is matching the song to the singer. If that's right, you just can't mess it up.

BACKGROUND VOCALS
TODD RUNDGREN,
NEARLY HUMAN
(WARNER BROTHERS RECORDS)
SCOTT MATHEWS, VOCALIST

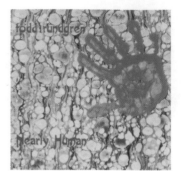

We walked into Studio D at Fantasy [Berkeley, California] without ever hearing the songs we were to record. This was somewhat nerve-wracking, because this album was recorded completely live: All the instruments, Todd's lead vocals, and our background vocals were going down together. However, Todd wanted our first impressions to be the last. We were divided into three groups of three, according to vocal ranges. The vocal arrangement was already recorded on a demo tape, and Todd showed each group their parts, then sent them away to rehearse to the tape. Within one hour after first hearing the song, we were in the studio cutting tracks live with the band.

The experience taught us that the intuitive approach to the song was usually right. The parts were extremely difficult— big lush chords and staggered melodies— and Todd said, "If you're going to make a mistake, make a loud mistake." The idea was to always sing like you meant it. If we messed up during a take we were told to confess. Of course, it took a while before everyone got everything right, and we recorded a number of takes. There was some pressure to get things down fast, as Todd was singing full-out, and the more takes he had to do, the more fatigued he got.

After we knew we had a take bagged, Todd instructed us to do a "mood-altered take." This meant we were free to express ourselves without being limited to the written part. In my case, that meant going full combo-plate crazy. The whole experience taught me a lot about how intuition and immediacy can energize a performance. In addition, the feeling of that many bodies in one room singing live was absolutely thrilling, and it definitely inspired some exciting performances.

THE PRODUCER'S ROLE
JANN ARDEN, A TIME FOR MERCY (A&M RECORDS)
ED CHERNEY, PRODUCER/ENGINEER

A&M Records sent me Jann's tape, and I was immediately captivated by her songs and voice. We're coming out of a period where not a lot of great songs were written, and I want to work with people who have something to say. In return, I feel I'm able to help an artist clear the way to get their best work on tape.

The sonic environment [of the record] was left up to me—Jann's demo was just acoustic guitar and voice—but production is always a collaboration. It's important to involve the artist in the process, because you certainly want, and need, their support.

I got kind of ballsy and decided to record the project almost completely live. Jann's songs defined the emotional quality of her work, so I put a band together that would be sympathetic to what she was trying to communicate. Jim Keltner played drums. He's amazing: He can actually play "sad," and he's the only drummer who ever asked me for a lyric sheet. David Resnick, who happens to be vice-president of A&R at Chameleon Records, played guitar—it was kind of nice having a record executive on the other side of the [control room] glass—as did Jann's regular guitarist, Bob Foster. Rounding out the group was Kenny Lyon on bass and C.J. Vanston on piano. As I said, everyone was recorded live, including Jann, who sang and played acoustic guitar simultaneously.

The scary thing was that there was no pre-production, because I wanted an almost improvisational environment. The idea was to put these characters in the studio and see what they'd do. We'd sit in a circle, and Jann would play the song a couple of times, then we'd set everyone up and start working it out. Three or four hours later, we'd have the song done.

The best part was that everyone was nervous and on their toes, and this is when those wonderful "mistakes" happen. I wanted to document the magic of the musicians and how they related to the artist and her material. I wasn't out to produce a slick record that sacrificed emotion. I believe that if you do too much pre-production, you can overlearn the song. Then, when you start recording, the actual performance becomes a technical exercise, like sawing wood.

MR. BONZAI/PACIFICBRIDGE

Jann Arden and Ed Cherney at Brooklyn studios in Los Angeles.

Working live with Jann, the musicians were forced to communicate more; they had to really listen to the song and react to it and each other. The interplay allowed certain "surprises" that helped to make this record something special.

BRINGING IT ON HOME

Although top recording engineers command state-of-the-art equipment, less technically endowed home recordists can still cop licks from the pros. For example, using composite vocal tracks—as David Frazer does with Whitney Houston—doesn't require an SSL console with automation. Wily recordists can employ SMPTE to sync analog rhythm tracks to a hard-disk recorder and perform as many takes as the software allows. In addition, anyone with access to two modular digital multitracks can use one machine for recording rhythm tracks and the other to stack and submix vocal performances. Even someone limited to a cassette 8-track can "final" mix rhythm tracks to DAT and re-record the stereo mix to two tracks of the multitrack. This procedure frees up six tracks for composite takes.

Solo performers can assemble a *faux* background chorus (*à la* Todd Rundgren) by taking some tips from Scott Mathews, a master at tracking one-person choirs.

"To assemble different vocal textures for a group sound, I record a number of takes on separate tracks and combine normal and altered performances," says Mathews. "I'll use the pitch control on my Tascam MS16 multitrack deck to speed up and slow down the tape. If I sing when the tape is sped up, it sounds like I've gained 40 pounds [when the deck is returned to normal speed]. When the tape is slowed down, I lose about ten years. Mic positioning is also helpful in masking the fact that one person is singing all the parts. Mix proximities—stand close to the mic for one take and a few steps back for another—and switch microphones to take advantage of different tonal characteristics."

Recording instruments often is a matter of experimenting with anarchy. Remember, imagination can transform limitations into genius. After all, how many engineers would use an SM57 to record a kick drum? Brendan O'Brien did it on the Red Hot Chili Peppers' *Blood Sugar Sex Magik*, and that album absolutely rips it up. (Be honest, how many of you thought a decent kick sound was possible only with an expensive, large-diapraghm microphone?) I've always thought that the two critical mantras for the heads-up producer/engineer should be "When in doubt, do whatever sounds right" and "If it sounds right, to hell with convention!"

Vernon Reid's Radical Lead Guitar

I THOUGHT I WAS UNSHOCKABLE.
Well, at least as far as musical gear is concerned. I have succumbed to personal equipment lust, witnessed myriad stacks and racks from the backstages of countless rock concerts, and drifted blissfully in the gadget universe that is the domain of an electronic musician. But I still wasn't prepared for the diagram that Sean Beresford, guitar tech for Living Colour's Vernon Reid, faxed me to illustrate the incendiary guitarist's rig.

The schematic is two pages long and about as far away from a simple "plug guitar into amp" setup as a Tonka truck is from the space shuttle. An effect as elementary as a Crybaby wah-wah coexists with MIDI patch bays, MIDI preamps, two guitar synths, assorted sound modules and samplers, digital signal processors, custom amp heads, and a vocoder. This ain't rock 'n' roll; this is "Johnny B. Goode" in the 25th century.

"Living Colour is a funny hybrid," admits Reid. "Because we're a rock band, it's important that we physically play our instruments. On the other hand, we have a wide-open attitude toward technology. Electronics are a huge part of my sound, and I don't believe they've diluted the guitar's power. Look at the techno scene; it's almost an 'anti-personality' cult of totally electronic dance music. But some of the tracks are real tough—almost hard-core—and there's an insane edge to everything. I think techno proves that there's no reason music can't be electronic *and* physical."

Some examples of Reid's marriage of technology and sensuality are the undulating symphonic lines underscoring the ethereal ballad "Nothingness" from Living Colour's recent album, *Stain*.

"Lately I've been influenced by ambient, droning bands, such as the Cocteau Twins and My Bloody Valentine," Reid explains. "So on 'Nothingness' I wanted a heavy, expansive ambience. And instead of having the guitar play clustered chords, I wanted to use cello-inspired melodic lines that would be thick enough to imply chords without actually playing them."

To attain the appropriate sonic density, Reid integrated the worlds of guitar and keyboard. His custom Hamer guitar (with a sustain feature built into the neck) is outfitted with conventional guitar pickups and a hex pickup. The straight guitar signal was routed into a TriAxis preamp and processed with an Eventide H3000. A "glassy" effect was achieved by using a harmonizing program—one unison part was mixed with a part one octave higher—with regeneration and delay. Amplification was handled via Mesa/Boogie Rectifier and 2/90 power amps, output to Mesa/Boogie

by Michael Molenda

and VHT 4 x 12 speaker cabinets.

The hex pickup was connected to a Gibson MAX guitar synth (for pitch-to-MIDI conversion) which controlled a Korg Wavestation A/D with a custom "Nothingness" patch that layered string and pad voices together. In addition, the Hall Strings program on an E-mu Proteus/1 was added to the aural stew. The synth voices roared through a VHT Red power amp and two Bag End 15-inch speaker cabinets.

"Pretty much what I gave the [recording] engineers is what's on the record," says Reid. "They just put a few mics around my speaker cabinet and tweaked the console EQ."

On *Stain,* Reid's quest for the cutting edge also unveiled a rather arcane instrument.

"On the bridge of 'Leave It Alone,' I didn't play a guitar *or* a keyboard," says Reid. "I used a prototype of an instrument called the Starr Datapump. It's a synth controller that's basically a guitar with keys instead of strings. It even has a joystick in place of a tremolo bar. In Guitar Mode, the Datapump acts just like a guitar, but because it's a purely MIDI instrument, there's no pitch-to-MIDI delay. I use it when I want more attack, because the Datapump lets you play as fast as you can fret the notes."

But, as the title of another song on *Stain* exclaims, the visionary Reid is "Never Satisfied."

"Do you ever wonder if technology is moving fast enough?" he asks. "I mean, even though the capabilities of the machines are more advanced than most people use, some things are still lagging. Believe me, as soon as they can get pitch-to-MIDI [conversion] working so you can really sweat on the guitar, I have plans."

•

Living Colour (Vernon Reid is second from right)

MARK LEIALOHA

Michael Hutchence's Vocal Irreverence

"IT SOUNDS HORRIBLE!" exclaimed Andrew Faulkner, a talented (albeit less-than-tactful) graphic designer and the former art director of *Electronic Musician*. Faulkner was reacting to the brutally compressed vocal on "Heaven Sent," the premiere single from INXS' *Welcome To Wherever You Are* album. "Michael Hutchence has such a great voice," he continued. "Why would they mess him up?"

Faulkner's reaction was rather funny, considering that his personal artistic vision routinely involves butchering stock images for arcane collages. Manipulation of known quantities into unique permutations is the fearless tradition of the creative arts. Picasso embraced this, as did Chuck Berry. And in today's pop music genre, bloated and fat with marketing niches and gelded playlists, it never hurts to shake things up a bit.

"We tried to break as many rules as possible," confesses producer Mark Opitz, who directed the mayhem of *Welcome To Wherever You Are*. "It was essential that the album possess a certain organic character—I call it 'true grit'—and passion took precedence over sonic quality. After all, we didn't make this record for other engineers and producers."

On "Heaven Sent," Hutchence's tortured vocal sets the tone for the album's gritty swagger. Opitz toured with INXS for a year, preparing and motivating the band to cut tracks with the relentless fury inherent in their live shows.

To ensure an explosive performance, Hutchence was recorded live with the entire band in the control room—minus the drummer, who was shuffled off to a proper studio room for isolation purposes—listening to huge monitor speakers at tremendous volumes. The vocal on the record is the first take. ("We weren't concerned about other instruments bleeding into the vocal mic," Opitz admits.)

Hutchence's voice was recorded with a Beyer M88 microphone, then routed through the onboard compressor on a SSL Series G console. The vocal's gnarled timbre was produced by setting the compression ratio at 20:1, with a fast attack and release. Further sonic damage was added by recording the voice with "telephone" EQ: Midrange frequencies were boosted drastically, and bass tones were rolled off. "Believe it or not, I would have preferred the vocal with even harsher EQ and buried even deeper in the mix than what ended up on the record," states Opitz.

by Michael Molenda

Ballads were treated more conventionally, and the silky resonance that bathes Hutchence's crooning on "Beautiful Girl" illustrates the versatility of compression. Hutchence sang the sparse ode to a runaway waif through a Neumann

U87 microphone (*sans* pop shield) routed into a Summit Audio TLA100 compressor. Because the TLA100 is basically an in/out device that reduces gain by 2 or 3 dB, the compression effect is very subtle. Placing Hutchence in a "dead" vocal booth and having him sing close to the mic produced an intimate quality that sounds as if the singer is whispering into one's ear.

"Sonically, we really tried to evoke 1960s 'album rock' productions that offered continuous listening experiences," says Opitz. "The last thing we wanted was an album with two huge hits and a bunch of other songs tossed in." •

INXS (Michael Hutchence is fourth from left)

Kitaro's Elements of Humanity

IN THE CURRENT VERNACULAR, "electronic musician" implies a specific breed of creator. And of course, the narrowest definition harvests the widest acceptance: a MIDI keyboardist or composer utilizing computer technology to painstakingly construct flawless musical works.

But what about a down-home blues guitarist plugging into a battered Fender Twin? Nothing computerized here, but Reddy Kilowatt is an essential partner in each and every lick. In a literal sense, anyone tapping into America's power grid to perform or record music is an electronic musician. The priests and priestesses of high technology are just another subculture within a large and artistically rich society. And regardless of one's stylistic "clubhouse," true visionaries harness technology to enhance creativity, not control it.

Sometimes that means taking a few steps backward.

"My technique is still analog," laughs internationally renowned recording artist (and electronic musician) Kitaro. "I use ancient synthesizers, and all my music is played by hand. I don't use sequencers. Yes, my music is sometimes not on the beat, but I am a human artist. I am not a machine."

The ancient analog instruments that comprise Kitaro's unique cross-cultural style include a Korg Poly-800, a Roland SH-01, and a Roland 330 vocoder. Even the environmental sounds of waterfalls and wind on Kitaro's album *Dream* (Geffen Records), are generated by analog synthesis. (Most artists rely on digital samples for these audio milieus.)

by Michael Molenda

"Analog synths have a special sound," explains Kitaro. "Even though the instrument is electronic, the sound has an organic timbre. These synths feel very natural and complement the way I program sounds. Every day is different, so the tones vary depending on my ears and physical condition. Sometimes this is a

KAZUNOBU YANAGI

Kitaro

problem when recording: Today's beautiful sound may appear very harsh tomorrow. But this uncertainty does not inhibit me. I like the way things are constantly developing."

On *Dream*, Kitaro combines his trademark electronic textures with acoustic instruments such as taiko drums, flute, tabla, and the distinctive voice of Yes crooner Jon Anderson. For Kitaro, arranging a sonic landscape invokes yet another human characteristic: intuition.

"I want to use all sounds: digital, analog, and classical," he says. "But I must be careful to make each sound serve the music. I usually compose a piece entirely on synthesizers, then I listen and decide what instruments should make the sounds. For this, I become one of the audience. You see, I have both sides. I am the composer, and I am a listener. If I feel good about a sound, then perhaps someone else will share that good feeling."

The organic, "human performance" ethic of Kitaro's music—and his reliance on battered analog synths—does not mean he shuns modern technology. It's simply a matter of putting the artist first.

"I'm learning to use computers, and I want to use new technology," Kitaro admits. "If I can put my spirit into a sequence or digital sound, if I can feel my spirit *through* the technology, then I can be true to my heart." •

Al Eaton's Big Boom Theory

FOR A NATION OF IMMIGRANTS raised amidst the crowded, clanging rhythm of the streets, Americans have a tough time getting down to their roots. In the 1950s, a cross-cultural musical gumbo called rock 'n' roll amplified the fears of the righteous, who heard sex and the devil in every beat. The feds shut down rock 'n' roll radio, tossed Chuck Berry in jail, and shipped Elvis off to Europe.

It wasn't until shrewd record men forged a pact with the "devil's music" that the abomination was able to flourish (a Faustian intrigue that turned these entrepeneurs into millionaires within months and created formidable American entertainment conglomerates).

Today, rap music is initiating an historical *déjà vu*. Once again, the rhythm of the streets is rising to embrace misguided youth, and middle-class America is not amused. Rap is the ethnic literature of modern urban society, a scatting bravado that fuses violence and hope and frustration and joy with the biggest beat pop music has ever produced. And the foundation of rap's mythic groove is the booming kick drum, defined by the Roland TR-808 drum machine.

"The TR-808 became a standard about the same time car stereos evolved into more powerful systems with subwoofers," explains producer Al Eaton, who remixed Kid Sensation's "Ride the Rhythm"

for a 12-inch vinyl single release on NASTYMIX Records. "The detuned 808 kick was perfect for showing off a [car stereo] system. You'd pull up next to somebody and let the rumble say, 'I've got more beat than you.'"

Eaton's remix of "Ride the Rhythm" used only the vocals from the original 24-track master tape. A completely new backing track was constructed atop a rhythmic stew of sampled TR-808 kicks, tuned differently for specific sections.

Building the track wasn't easy. Kid's 1-inch master tape had to be transferred to the professional 2-inch format before Eaton could work with it. During this procedure, the SMPTE time code was not refreshed, and when Eaton received the tape, he couldn't sync up his MIDI gear. Ultimately, the vocals were sampled section by section and "flown into" the new rhythm track. In addition, the lengths of the drum samples were manipulated in Digidesign's *Sound Tools*. All the samples were triggered "dry"—without signal processing—to ensure that the beats "hit real hard."

by Michael Molenda

"A lot of times I prefer not to use the big-boom 808 kick, because now it's like putting catsup on everything you eat," admits Eaton. "Sometimes, to get an early 1980s sound, I'll use an actual 808 drum machine. However, because the 808 is analog, the sound is unstable: Every time it hits, the tone changes a little. For more contemporary tracks, it's better to use samples, because the sound is always right there."

However, Eaton's remix did more than just slam a better groove. His rearrangement earned him songwriting credit on the track—a measure of clout usually reserved for proven hitmakers.

"I was grateful NASTYMIX offered me a writing credit," says Eaton. "They feel my remix makes the track more accessible to radio and video. What I did was give the track the 'Oakland Sound,' a slower, more laid-back style that's a bit sexier than the original (album cut) version that was real street-sounding. Luckily for me and Kid, the Oakland Sound was real hot when the remix came out." •

Al Eaton

Kyuss' Ambient Aggression

EVERY ONCE IN A WHILE, an album bubbles up from the quagmire of sonically cloned record productions to remind us that the roots of pop music are regional. Years ago, all the sweat and soul of places like Motown, Memphis, Philly, and L.A. were forged into record grooves. The music evoked the cities that spawned it, and you could pinpoint an artist's zip code by the sound of his or her record. Today, it seems as if all the big-hair bands on MTV live in the same house (or at least share one guitar and a snare drum).

Such homogenization makes *Blues for the Red Sun* by Kyuss (Dali Records) one of those rare regional records, a sonic document of a band and its environment. The kick is that it's not an urban translation of rock 'n' roll angst: Kyuss hails from the upscale surburban desert community of Palm Springs, California. And making desert music in the closed, controlled environment of the recording studio meant rethinking the conventional method of close-miking instruments for optimum tone and separation.

"The desert has a strange effect on our music, because there's no sense of boundaries," says Kyuss guitarist Josh Homme. "When we discussed making the album with [producer] Chris Goss, ambient recording seemed the only way to get the expansive sound we wanted. To achieve this, we turned entire rooms into 'speakers,' and took over the whole studio, from the hallways to the coffee room. It was hell working there when Kyuss was around."

Blues for the Red Sun was tracked with the rhythm section playing together (singer John Garcia recorded his vocals in an isolation booth) in the main studio at Sound City (Van Nuys, California). The room is a perfect environment for ambient sonics, measuring 40 x 40 feet with a 25-foot-high ceiling and wooden floors. Drummer Brant Bjork set up his kit in the middle of the studio, and room mics were positioned to take full advantage of the space's natural reverb. As insurance, the kit was close-miked as well. However, except for a touch of the close snare mic to add punch, only the sound of the room mics is on the record.

Homme's guitar rig was blocked off inside a 10 x 10-foot hallway alcove that normally serves as a rest area. His *by Michael Molenda* two Ampeg V4 speaker cabinets were placed on top of a couch, and five mics were placed "wherever they picked up the best sound." The mic positioning proved so ideal that the guitar timbre on the record is a virtual document of the amp and the natural room acoustics; only minimal EQ was employed to process the source sound.

Finally, the bass cabinet was baffled inside a 15-foot doorway, with three mics positioned around the space. Once again, the miked sound proved to be so good that a direct signal recorded as a "safety" was not used.

"We approached *Blues for the Red Sun* the way a rock 'n' roll record should be made," contends Homme. "We finished the record in fourteen days, and most of the tracks are first takes. Some critics hate the record's production because it sounds too live, but that sound *is* Kyuss. This is a band that started out playing 'generator parties' in the desert. The wide-open spaces are as much a part of our music as the instruments we play."   •

KURT MUNDAHL

Kyuss

The Anatomy
of a Break

FIRST CAME THE SONG. Well, more accurately, first came the personal tragedy that inspired the song.

Nancie De Ross, an unsigned San Francisco solo artist, retreated inside her tiny apartment to mourn the end of a relationship. One of the fruits of her sorrow was the song "I Don't Know Why." The melancholy ballad ultimately found its way onto the soundtrack of *Fathers and Sons,* a film starring Jeff Goldblum. Now, anyone will tell you that it is almost impossible for an unsigned, unknown artist to score a track on a major movie soundtrack. This is the story of a miracle.

"I had broken up with my boyfriend, and I was feeling this incredible loneliness and fear," says De Ross. "But I didn't want to distract myself from the pain. I thought about all the great, sad ballads, and 'I Don't Know Why' came out of me completely written—lyrics and music—in about five minutes. I never changed a thing."

As fate would have it, an A&M Records executive saw De Ross open a concert for Todd Rundgren and offered her $3,000 to record a development demo for the label. Finally given enough of a budget to "do things right," De Ross chose James Wilsey, the evocative guitarist who helped define Chris Isaak's sound, to produce the project.

"I Don't Know Why" and two other compositions were recorded in Wilsey's home MIDI studio. Song arrangements were sequenced on Mark of the Unicorn's *Performer,* and the final MIDI tracks and De Ross' voice were recorded into a hard-disk recorder (Digidesign's Deck).

"I just came in and sang the vocal right in Jimmy's apartment," she says. "If you listen hard, you can hear traffic in the background."

Wilsey played the completed demo for a friend, Jim Dunbar, who also happens to be an executive with Sony Music. Dunbar liked "I Don't Know Why" enough to champion the song to director Paul Mones, who was making *Fathers and Sons* for Pacific Pictures (a division of Sony Entertainment). Mones not only put the song in the film (and on the soundtrack album), he used the very demo track that was recorded and mixed in Wilsey's apartment. Of course, none of this happened overnight.

"I was chewing up my fingernails for about a year *by Michael Molenda* and a half waiting to hear if the song made it into the movie," says De Ross. "I read about it in a local music paper before anyone told me a thing. That's how much they (the label executives) communicate with artists."

The big payday is yet to come. Sony gave De Ross an artist royalty advance of $500 and an additional $500 advance for writing the song. She also is entitled to 1/11 of the sales royalties set aside for the eleven artists on the soundtrack album.

"Basically, I've earned enough money from this deal to buy some toothpaste," jokes De Ross.

EPILOGUE

Unfortunately, the limited distribution of *Fathers and Sons* didn't exactly propel the soundtrack album towards the top of the charts. No artist on the compilation broke out with a mainstream hit. That was bad news for De Ross; Dunbar had said he'd consider signing her (to Sony Music) if her track generated some heat. The A&M deal also faded away, but De Ross is philosophical about her fluctuating fortunes.

"The next break will come whenever it's ready," she says. "But I'm not sitting idle waiting for it, either. I'm constantly writing and performing, and I intend to

Nancie De Ross

cut some more tracks with Jimmy. I'm just happy this [soundtrack] was finally released, because it was like holding a baby inside me for a year and a half." •